1-2-3 Magic

Training Your Children to Do
What *You* Want!

1-2-3 Magic

Thomas W. Phelan, Ph.D.

CHILD MANAGEMENT INC

Glen Ellyn, Illinois

Cover design and illustrations by Margaret Mayer
Cover photography by Steve Orlick
Child Management Logo by Steve Roe

Printed in the United States of America
10 9 8 7 6 5 4 3 2 1

For more information, contact:
Child Management, Inc.
800 Roosevelt Road
Glen Ellyn, Illinois 60137

Publisher's Cataloging in Publication
(Prepared by Quality Books Inc.)

Phelan, Thomas W., 1943-
    1-2-3 magic: training your children to do what you want! /
Thomas W. Phelan. — 2nd ed.
    p. cm.
    ISBN 0-9633861-2-3

    1. Discipline of children,   I. Title. II. Title:
One-two-three magic.

HQ770.4.P44 1994   649'.64
                            QBI94-1214

to
Eileen

Contents

Part III: No Child Will Thank You

Part IV: Encouraging Good Behavior

Part V: More Serious Stop Behavior

Part VI: Your Child's Self-Esteem

Part VII: Over the Years

Part VIII: Counting for Teachers

Part IX: Final Thoughts

Preface to the Second Edition

The very first *1-2-3 Magic* seminar took place at a local Holiday Inn on a cold April day in 1984. It was attended by twenty-eight parents.

That was eighty thousand books, twenty thousand videos, and six hundred seminars ago. Today the 1-2-3 method is rapidly becoming one of the most popular child rearing programs in the country. We believe there are two basic reasons for this. First, it is very easy to learn. Second, it works.

The basic methods were developed over the period of years after the author got his doctorate, which was also about the time he became a father. What followed then were years and years of trial and error learning, both in the role of parent and in the role of therapist trying to help other parents manage their own children.

This experimentation was not, of course, completely without guidance. Graduate school books and courses had taught some useful principles, such as positive reinforcement, active listening and operant conditioning. What had to be discovered from scratch, however, were the critical child-rearing principles that make *1-2-3 Magic* unique: the "little adult assumption," the distinction between "Start" and "Stop" behavior, the "No-Talking, No-Emotion" Rules, the six kinds of Testing and Manipulation, and the exact details of the counting procedure itself.

These essential pieces came from the seemingly interminable process of sending parents home with an assignment, having them come back and report how it worked, agreeing on modifications, trying out the new tactics, coming back, tuning it up again, and so on. Family after family after family. Although the process was at times tedious, it also involved the excitement of discovery and finally the satisfaction of seeing the end result begin to work again and again and again.

From this crucible of collaboration, repeated experimentation and hard work came a product which will stand the test of time.

The first people, therefore, to whom we owe a debt of gratitude are the parents whose struggles helped develop *1-2-3 Magic* in the years before 1984. And let's also not forget their children, who served as our first "experimental subjects."

Also critical to this development was the cooperation and patience of my wife, Eileen, and, of course, the fun and the challenges presented to us at home by our two children, Tom and Julie.

Had too few patients come through the office, the 1-2-3 might never have materialized. But two long time friends and pediatricians, Roy Betti and Ron Eriksen, long ago saw to it that we wouldn't lack for work. Collaborating with them over the years in a spirit of openmindedness and cooperation was invaluable.

Before the age of computers the original 1-2-3 book had to be typed by hand. This job was accomplished with skill and precision by Nancy Roe, who has also provided skillful assistance with the horrible task of proofreading. The present version of the 1-2-3 has also been honed during the process of giving hundreds and hundreds of workshops, which were set up by Peggy Farrell. Her organizational skills and conscientiousness have always made them run smoothly. In both designing the books and in marketing them, the energy and expertise of Jana Larkin has been extremely helpful.

Four new chapters for teachers, covering preschool to junior high, have been added to the second edition. These have been based on the actual experiences of school personnel, and they should be very helpful to those who wish to use the 1-2-3 in school settings. Thanks here go to Debbie Cook, Jan Cernock, Helen Callahan, Chuck Swangren, Paula Rancilio, Susan Lawson, Frances Wilson, Tricia Goodell, Theresa Ouderkirk, and Claire Taylor. With their help, these new chapters are down-to-earth and practical.

Applications of the 1-2-3 in community mental health centers have also added a lot to our knowledge of the usefulness of the program. Our thanks especially to the DuPage County Mental Health Center (Illinois), which for years has taught an expanded eight session version of *1-2-3 Magic* called "Parents in Charge." In Canada, Team Leader Sig Taylor of the Young Children's Development Program of the Southeastern Alberta Health Unit has found a way to use the 1-2-3 to dramatically reduce intake overload and waiting lists for child evaluations.

Finally, thanks are due to Andy Olcott of Booklet Publishing Company for his advice, hard work and helpful suggestions over the years.

Due to the combined efforts of all these people, the *1-2-3 Magic* dream has become a reality.

How to Use This Book

The book that follows describes some very effective methods for managing the behavior of children from the ages of approximately two to twelve years old. To get the best results, several things should be kept in mind:

1. The methods must be used exactly as they are described here, especially with regard to the No-Talking and No-Emotion Rules.

2. If both parents are living at home, they should both use the techniques.

3. Single parents can use the methods well by themselves.

4. Grandparents, babysitters and other caregivers have also found the 1-2-3 very helpful in managing young children. In fact, many grandparents have first discovered *1-2-3 Magic* on their own and then shared it with their children.

5. Any possible physical problems in the kids should have been ruled out.

Psychological counseling is indicated *before* using the methods in this book if any child has a history of excessive separation anxiety, physical violence, or extremely self-punitive behavior. These children can be exceptionally difficult to manage during the initial testing period when they are still adjusting to the new discipline. If a family is currently in counseling, the book should be discussed with the counselor before being used.

Psychological evaluation and counseling are indicated *after* using the procedures described here if:

1. Marital instability or conflict are interfering with the effective use of the methods.

2. One or both parents are incapable of following the No-Talking and No-Emotion Rules.

3. Testing and Manipulation are continuing at a high level for more than three weeks.

Chapters 1-11 *must* be read before using the 1-2-3, and it is preferable that they also be read before using the methods in Chapters 12-28.

In this second edition of *1-2-3 Magic* there are a number of new chapters. In addition to the four chapters for teachers, the new chapters also include "What to Do in Public," "Active Listening," "Active Listening and Counting," and "10 Steps for Building Self-Esteem." Other chapters have been extensively rewritten. The chapter on homework, for example, has lots of new ideas and the examples of using the 1-2-3 ("Counting in Action") are all new.

We believe these changes will make the second edition of *1-2-3 Magic* an even more valuable resource for parents, teachers, and others who care for our children.

What's the Problem?

Family Fun

"I'm not talking to you anymore until you finish your entire dinner—the meatloaf *and* the vegetables."

"Why?"

"Cause you're just sitting there fooling around. We will talk when you're done."

"That's stupid."

"Don't give me that, young man. And I don't care for that attitude. Now that's the last I want to hear from you till you've eaten."

"That's not fair. How come you never had this silly rule for Emily or anyone else around here?"

"Your sister has nothing to do with this!"

"Why are you always picking on me?"

"BE QUIET AND EAT! If you want to go out and play tonight or at any time for the rest of your life!"

"I don't care if I do or not."

1

Family Trouble

No one ever said parenting (or teaching) was easy. Living with young children can be one of life's most enjoyable experiences. It can also become unbelievably frustrating if you don't quite know what you're doing.

There are those days when it seems that half the time the kids are doing what you *don't want* them to do, and the other half of the time they're not doing what you *do want* them to do.

It's also easy to forget that it is impossible to give kids everything that they want. Raising and educating children means that, in addition to nurturing and supporting them, you must also frustrate them on a regular basis—for their own good and for the good of everyone. But when they are frustrated, kids seem to instinctively have a knack for getting their parents or teachers into troublesome sidetracks that can eliminate fun, destroy affection and—over the long run—ruin relationships.

Repeat the dinner table scene above a thousand times and you have guaranteed misery. That's no way for anyone to live and certainly no way for a child to grow up.

Children don't come with a training manual. Adults, therefore, need to know how to handle children's difficult behavior, how to encourage their good behavior, and how to handle the inevitable sidetrack of testing and manipulation. This must be done in a manner that is fair, perfectly clear, and not abusive. This may be a difficult task, but it is critical to peaceful coexistence. It is also critical to each child's ability to enjoy life and maintain healthy self-esteem.

Part I:

Straight Thinking

Welcome to
the 1-2-3

1-2-3 Magic will teach you some very simple, precise, and effective ways to manage your children in approximately the two to twelve year old age range. The methods that will be described are very easy to learn. You do not have to be a saint, genius, or professional psychotherapist in order to use them properly. Too many parenting books simply tell you seventy-five more things that you aren't doing with your kids, then leave you feeling guilty with no clear place to start.

When you finish with the "1-2-3," you will know exactly what to do, what not to do, what to say, and what not to say in just about every one of the common, everyday problem situations you will run into with your kids. You will also know how to handle more serious difficulties. You will also find that, if you use the 1-2-3 correctly, it will work! It has been shown to be very effective with two to twelve year olds, whether they are "problem" children or just average youngsters. *1-2-3 Magic* has been used successfully with learning disabled, attention deficit, and emotionally disturbed children, as well as with the visually and hearing impaired.

When you finish reading *1-2-3 Magic* (or watching the video), it is a good idea to start immediately. Talk it over with your spouse, if both parents are living at home, and then get going right away. If you are a single parent, take a deep breath and then get started. If you don't, you may never get around to it.

If you do start right away, things will change fast. There is good news and bad news here. The good news is that about one half of the kids will immediately fall into the "immediate cooperator" category. You just relax and enjoy that. The bad news is that the other half will be "immediate testers." They are going to take it to you to see if you are serious and really mean business. If you stick to your guns, you can usually get this group shaped up pretty well in about a week to ten days.

Believe it or not, you might have a much more peaceful home, more enjoyable kids, and better self-esteem—all in the foreseeable future!

Before we get into the details of the 1-2-3, we must clarify two very important concepts:

1. The two categories of problem behavior (Chapter 2).
2. The dangerous assumption parents (and teachers) make about children (Chapter 3).

2

Start & Stop Behavior

W hen you are having problems with your kids, they are, in general doing one of two kinds of things. They are either 1) doing something you don't want them to do, or which you want them to *stop*, or 2) they are not doing something you would like them to *start* doing. Therefore we call these two kinds of things "*Stop*" behavior and "*Start*" behavior.

Stop behaviors include the frequent, minor everyday hassles kids get into, such as arguing, whining, fighting, pouting, temper tantrums, disrespect, yelling, and so on. Each thing by itself isn't so bad, but add them all up and by the end of the day you may feel like hitchhiking to Seattle!

Start behaviors include things like cleaning rooms, homework, practicing obnoxious musical instruments, getting up and out in the morning, bedtime, eating, and the like. Here you want the child to do something good.

The reason for distinguishing between these two kinds of behaviors is this: you will use different tactics for each type.

Here's how it works:

• For **Stop Behavior** such as...

> arguing
> fighting
> screaming
> tantrums
> teasing

you will use the 1-2-3, or "counting," proce-dure.

(Chapter 5)

• For **Start Behavior** such as...

> eating
> doing homework
> going to bed
> cleaning rooms
> getting up and out in the morning

you will have a choice of six tactics (or combinations of them):

> 1. Sloppy PVF
> 2. Kitchen Timers
> 3. The Docking System
> 4. Natural Consequences
> 5. Charting
> 6. A variation of the 1-2-3
> (Chapter 12)

When dealing with some trouble with a child, therefore, you will need to first determine if you have a Stop or a Start problem. If you mix up your tactics (e.g., use counting for homework), you will not get as good results—or you may get no results at all.

You must also think realistically—and not wishfully—about your kids. You may have a dangerous, false assumption floating around in your head regarding your children.

3

The Little Adult Assumption

Many parents and teachers have an idea in their heads about
kids that causes a lot of trouble. This false assumption leads either
to discipline attempts that don't work, or to stormy scenes that make
everyone feel bad. This erroneous idea about children is known as the
"little adult assumption."

The little adult assumption is the idea that kids are just smaller than
we are, but they have hearts of gold and are basically reasonable and
unselfish. If your child is not doing his homework, you simply sit him
down and explain to him the three golden, irrefutable reasons why he
should. First, he will learn more. Second, it will make you and his teacher
happy. And third, he will grow up to be a responsible and successful
person.

The child, naturally, after receiving this wealth of wisdom, responds
by saying, "Gee, I never looked at it like that before," and he immediately
goes to his room to complete his work.

Or imagine your eight year old son is torturing his little sister for the
fortieth time since they both got home from school. You ask him how he
would feel if someone did that to him all the time. He says, "You know,

11

you're right, I wouldn't like it very much. How insensitive I've been," and he stops—permanently.

This would certainly be nice, but it just doesn't happen. Kids are not little adults. But parents and teachers who believe—or want to believe—this myth are going to rely heavily on *words and reasons* in dealing with the kids and trying to change their behavior. And words and reasons are going to be miserable failures too much of the time. Sometimes they will have absolutely no impact at all. Other times they will take the parent and child through the *Talk-Persuade-Argue-Yell-Hit Syndrome.*

Your child is doing something you don't like. You try telling him why he shouldn't do it. He doesn't respond, so you start trying to persuade him to see things your way. When persuasion fails, you start arguing. Arguing leads to a yelling match, and when that fails, you may feel there is nothing left to do but hit. Actually, 90% of spankings and the like are simply parental temper tantrums.

We're not implying here that you are going around hitting your kids all the time. It may be true, however, that one of the main causes of child abuse (physical, not sexual) in this country is the little adult assumption. It is a parent who read in a book somewhere that talking was the way to go. Then, when talking and reasoning fail, the parent goes crazy and starts hitting, because they are extremely frustrated and don't know what else to do.

So kids are kids—not little adults. One writer, in fact, stated once that "Childhood is a period of transitory psychosis." That means that kids, when they are little, are sort of nuts! They are born unreasonable and selfish, and it is our job to help them become the opposite.

How do you do that? You start by changing your thinking about children. This may sound a little strange at first, but instead of thinking of your kids as little adults, think of yourself as a *Wild Animal Trainer*! This does not mean using whips, guns, or chairs. But what a wild animal trainer does, seriously, is choose a method—which is largely nonverbal—and repeat it until the "trainee" does what he wants. Our job in *1-2-3 Magic* is to present some useful training methods to you, then you repeat them until the trainees, your children, do what you want them to. Fortunately, you do not usually have to repeat these things forever and ever.

Dictatorship to Democracy

For those who are a little uncomfortable with this, thinking that it may be a little too heavy handed, the overall philosophy of *1-2-3 Magic* is what you might call "dictatorship to democracy." That means that when your kids are little, your house should be a dictatorship where you are the judge and jury. When the kids are in their mid to late teens, however, things should be more of a democracy, where the youngsters have more to say about the rules and policies that affect them. Even then, though, when push comes to shove, who's paying the mortgage? You are. And who knows better than they do what's good for them? You do, and you have a right (and duty) to impose that on them sometimes, even if they don't like it.

What if you have children who do respond to words and reasons? You are certainly lucky! Recent research has indicated that there are three such children in the United States, but if you do have one or more of them, you may not need this book. Or, if at times they stop responding to logic, you can consider using the 1-2-3.

The Two
Biggest Mistakes

The two biggest mistakes that parents and teachers make in dealing with children are: Too Much Talking and Too Much Emotion. We just finished discussing why all the talking is bad. It either doesn't work, or it takes you through the *Talk-Persuade-Argue-Yell-Hit Syndrome*.

Why is too much emotion destructive? It has to do with the fact that when they are little, little kids feel inferior. They feel inferior because they *are* inferior. Sure, they can be cute and nice and lovable, but they are also smaller, less privileged, less intelligent, less skillful, less responsible, and less of just about everything than their parents and the older kids. And this bugs them a lot! They don't like it. They do like to feel they are powerful and capable of making some mark on the world.

Have you ever seen a small child go down to a lake and throw rocks in the water? They can do that for hours, partly because the big splashes are a sign of their impact. They are making that happen.

What does this have to do with what happens at home? Simple. If this small child can get big old you all upset, your upset is the big splash for him. It's not that he has no conscience and is going to grow up to be a criminal. It's just that having all that power temporarily rewards—or feels

15

good to—the inferior part of the child. Parents who often say, "It drives me absolutely crazy when he eats his dinner with his fingers. Why does he do that?", may have already answered their own question. He may do that at least partly *because it drives them crazy.*

So a corollary of this is: if you have a child who is doing something you don't like, get real upset about it on a regular basis and, sure enough, he'll repeat it for you. There are certainly other discipline systems other than the 1-2-3, but you can ruin any of them for sure by talking too much and getting too excited. These two mistakes, of course, usually go hand in hand, and the emotion involved is usually anger.

Some parents can turn off the talking and the emotional upset like a faucet, and others have to work like dogs to get the job done. Even then, they often have to remind themselves over and over that talking and arguing and yelling and screaming don't really help. These tactics only blow off steam for a few seconds. If a parent finds that they can't shake these habits, some sort of outpatient counseling or psychotherapy is indicated.

Part II:

Controlling Obnoxious Behavior

5

The 1-2-3

S o, if the wild animal trainer model does not allow too much
talking and too much emotion, how exactly does it work? The model
we'll discuss here will be the 1-2-3, but there are two things that must be
said about it before we describe how it works.

*First of all, you will use the 1-2-3, or counting method, to deal with
Stop behaviors.* In other words, you will be counting things like arguing,
fighting, whining, yelling, tantrums, etc. You will not use it to get the child
to go to bed or practice the violin.

*Second, after you hear how to do the 1-2-3, you are likely to be
skeptical.* It may seem too easy to you, or you may feel like saying, "Hey,
buddy, you don't know my kid—this kid is a wild man!" Don't worry if
you feel this way; the 1-2-3 is deceptively simple and easy, but it is also
very powerful as long as you follow the No-Talking and No-Emotion
Rules. Many parents finish the book or video and feel skeptical. Then they
go home and try it, and they come back and say, "I can't believe it, it
worked like magic!"

There is no magic in *1-2-3 Magic*. It simply represents the careful,
logical, and persistent extension of certain common sense ideas and

behavioral principles in the discipline and training of children.

But don't worry if you are skeptical or have questions. We will attempt to answer all of your questions in a few chapters, and then you can begin.

So how does the 1-2-3 work? Imagine you have a four year old child (which many of you do). He is having a major temper tantrum on the kitchen floor at 6 PM because you wouldn't give him any potato chips right before dinner. He is banging his head on the floor, kicking the cabinets for all he's worth, and screaming bloody murder. You are at a loss for what to do.

You recall that your pediatrician told you to ignore it. Your mother told you to put a cold washcloth over his face. And your husband told you to beat the daylights out of him!

None of these are acceptable alternatives. With the 1-2-3, you hold up one finger, look down at the little devil, and say, "That's 1."

He doesn't care. He's insane with rage and keeps his tantrum going full force. So you let a few seconds go by, then hold up two fingers and say, That's 2." Same reaction. So after a few more seconds, you hold up three fingers and say, "That's 3, take 5." This means that he has had two chances to shape up and he blew it—he didn't shape up. So he goes off to his room for a "rest period" or "time out." (Some of you are wondering, "How do I get him there!?" We'll talk about that later.)

The child serves the time out. (By the way, a good rule of thumb for the length of the time out is one minute for each year of the child's life; 5 year old gets five minutes, ten year old 10, etc.) When the child comes out from the rest period, nothing at all is said about what happened, unless it is absolutely necessary.

You do not say, for example, "Now, are you going to be a good boy? Why do we have to go through this every day? I've told you a thousand times that you can't eat right before dinner, but you never seem to listen to me. Now you know your sister doesn't behave that way, and your father's going to be home any minute now, so you don't want to...blah, blah, blah..."

You simply be quiet and drop it. If the child does something else that's countable, feel perfectly free to count it. What will happen after a while is that you'll get good control—believe it or not —at 1 or 2. Some kids will always take you to 2, prompting some parents to say, "Don't you think he's manipulating us, always taking it to 2?" The answer is, "No he's not manipulating you always taking you to 2." What really drives people crazy is 10, or 20, or a child that has to be told 45 times before he'll shape up. Two times is not bad at all, and if the child hits 3, he's gone.

Other parents ask, with good reason, "What if the kid does something that's so bad, you don't want him to have three chances to do it?" For example, what if your child hits you? Your kids can't hit you. If your child hits you, it would be ludicrous to say, "That's 1" and give him two more shots. So if the thing is bad enough to begin with, you simply say, "That's three, take 5 and add 10 more for the seriousness of the offense."

What if your child called you a bad name he had just learned on the playground. Same thing. "That's 3, take 5, and add 10 more for the rotten mouth." And perhaps when that youngster returns from time out, an explanation would be in order about what the word meant and why he can't use it.

The No-Talking and No-Emotion Rules

Some people say something like, "Hey, we've used this counting stuff and it just doesn't work for us. Counting is just no good." Ninety plus percent of the time the problem here is very easy to detect: the people are not really using the 1-2-3 properly. Here's how their scene with their kid might go if they were back dealing with our four year old temper tantrum artist:

> "That's 1. Come on now, I'm getting a little sick and tired
> of this. I don't know why you can't do just one little thing for
> me—LOOK AT ME WHEN I'M TALKING TO YOU!—
> when we're always doing everything for you."
> "OK, that's 2! One more and you're history, young man. Do
> you really enjoy going to your room or do you just get a kick
> out of trying to drive me nuts!?" (Pause for breath)
> "OK, I'VE HAD IT! THAT'S 3! GET OUT OF MY SIGHT!
> TOMORROW WE'RE TALKING NEAREST ORPHAN-
> AGE! BEAT IT!"

Who's Responsible?

That's not the 1-2-3. It is, however, a major violation of our two cardinal rules: No-Talking and No-Emotion. An interesting thing happens when you keep talking like that. When you start out with "That's 1," the ball's in the kid's court. They're responsible by themselves for changing their behavior. But if you keep talking, a funny thing happens. You take over that responsibility, and the whole discipline scene changes. The rule now is they don't have to shape up unless you can produce one or more valid (acceptable to them) reasons why they should. It will usually be a cold day in hell before the average frustrated child in this situation mellows out because of your words, then sees the light and says, "Gee, I never looked at it like that before!"

Two other problems occur if parents violate our two cardinal rules. One is that the child can't clearly hear or pick out the warning ("That's 1") when it's mixed up with all the rest of that verbal garbage. If you have a child with Attention Deficit Disorder who doesn't pay attention very well in the first place, their attending to the warning only may become a hopeless proposition.

Another problem is that when you yell and nag and argue at a youngster, many of them will take it as a challenge and you will have a war on your hands. There are plenty of kids who would sooner cut off their left leg than lose a good fight. Unwise attempts on your part at talking or persuading *are guaranteed to take the child's focus off the possibility of good behavior and put their focus on the possibility of an enjoyable argument.*

So if the child is acting up, it's "That's 1 (button your lip)," "That's 2 (quiet)," and so on.

Sometimes your silence can speak louder than your words.

The Famous Twinkie Example

Our famous twinkie example will help you better understand the workings of the 1-2-3. This is a situation most of you parents have experienced in one way or another. You are cooking dinner at 5:45 PM and your eight year old daughter walks in the kitchen:

"Can I have a twinkie?"

"No, dear."

"Why not?"

"Because we're eating at six o'clock."

So far, so good, right? One explanation, if necessary, is fine. The problem is that most kids are not going to leave it there; they're going to press it further by adding something like, "Yeah, but I want one (sort of whiney)." So what are you going to do?

We are going to play this situation through three ways. In Scene I, the mother will try to handle the child and Mom believes the little adult assumption: words and reasons will change this kid's behavior. We'll see what happens with that.

In Scene II, the mother will be wising up. She will be starting to use the 1-2-3, but the child won't be used to it yet, and you'll see what happens with that.

In Scene III, the mother will still be using the 1-2-3, and the girl will have grown more accustomed to it.

Scene I: Starring the mother who believes in words and reason:

"Can I have a twinkie?"

"No, dear."

"Why not?"

"Cause we're eating at six o'clock."

"Yeah, but I want one."

"I just told you you couldn't have one."

"You never give me anything."

"What do you mean I never give you anything? Do you have
   clothes on? Is there a roof over your head? Am I feeding
   you in two seconds!?"

"You gave my brother one a half hour ago."

"Listen, are you your brother? And besides, he eats his
   dinner."

"I promise I'll eat my dinner."

"Don't give me this promise, promise, promise stuff, Heather!

"Yesterday—4:30 in the afternoon, you had half a peanut
    butter and jelly sandwich and you didn't eat anything at dinner!"
"THEN I'M GOING TO KILL MYSELF AND THEN
    RUN AWAY FROM HOME!!"
"WELL BE MY GUEST. I'M SICK OF THIS!!"

This is no good at all, but it is where trying to talk at the wrong time
can get you. Now Mom gets smart and starts using the 1-2-3, but it's in the
beginning and the child is still getting used to it.

Scene II: Starring mother beginning to use the 1-2-3:

"Can I have a twinkie?"
"No, dear."
"Why not?"
"Because we're eating at six o'clock."
"Yeah, but I want one."
"That's 1."
"You never give me anything!"
"That's 2."
"THEN I'M GOING TO KILL MYSELF AND THEN
    RUN AWAY FROM HOME!!"
"That's 3, take 5."

Mom did well. The child disappears for a rest period and the scene
is over. How's it going to go after a while, when the child is more used to
it and is realizing that testing and manipulation is useless?

Scene III: The 1-2-3 after a few days:

"Can I have a twinkie?"
"No, dear."
"Why not?"
"Because we're eating at six o'clock."
"Yeah, but I want one."
"That's 1."
(Pause) "Oh, all right." (Grumpy exit from kitchen)

This is fine, and you don't have to count the grumpy "Oh, all right" because it's not so bad and the child is leaving. If the child said, "Oh, all right, stupid jerk!", it would be an automatic 3 and off to the room.

What's Good about the 1-2-3?

The 1-2-3 will save you a lot of breath—and a lot of aggravation. One explanation—if absolutely necessary, and then you count. There is no extra talking and no extra emotion, and these two things, of course, go hand in hand. You stay calmer and it feels good when you get a good response at 1 or 2.

Also, your authority is not negotiable. It shouldn't be. You are the boss, and, as a matter of fact, you as the parent must frustrate your kids on a regular basis because you can't possibly give them everything they want. Many parents, though, complicate their discipline by setting for themselves two goals: the first goal is to discipline the children, and *the second goal is to get the kids to like it!* Like the mother in Scene I, the parent talks and talks and talks, waiting for the youngster to say, "Gee, I never looked at it like that before," and then happily give up the battle.

That doesn't usually happen. If the child does listen, and the talking seems to help, that's fine. But with a frustrated child that is not usually the case, and too often the talking graduates to arguing.

A final thing that helps with the 1-2-3 is that the punishment is short and sweet: about one minute per year of their life. This does not make the child so mad that when they come out they want war. With this regime, many kids come back from time out and just forget about it. And remember, you are not allowed to bring up what happened unless it is absolutely necessary.

When is it absolutely necessary? In those instances where the problem involved is something that the child definitely does not already understand, where what they did is something that is unusual and fairly serious, or where you really need more information from them about it.

The 1-2-3 is also easy enough that you can train babysitters and grandparents and other caretakers to use it. In fact, you should definitely do this so the kids get the same message from everyone.

The 1-2-3 can appear almost too simple. It is pretty straightforward, but raising kids is never an easy job. At this point your mind is probably filled with quite a few questions.

Let's take a look at some of the important ones that have come up most frequently over the years.

6

Common Questions

How long do you take in between counts?

Just long enough to allow the child time to shape up, or about 3 to 5 seconds. You're not going to give the child half an hour to continue the tantrum before you hit him with the 2. However, you would not say "That's 1" at nine in the morning, "That's 2" at eleven, and "That's 3, take 5" at three o'clock. The reason is that kids' time perspective is about five minutes forward and five back. So we have what we call our *20 Minute Rule:* if the child does three things wrong in any twenty minute period, you count him up to three. But if he does one thing, twenty minutes pass, and then he does something else, you go back to one. Very few children will get manipulative with this, like doing one thing, allowing twenty minutes to pass, and then figuring, "Now I get a free one!"

Note: many teachers do not use the 20 Minute Rule because—with twenty-five children in your class—it potentially allows for too much misbehavior in too short a period of time. Instead, the rule is expanded to cover a whole class period or even half of the day, depending on the ages of the kids.

Does the 1-2-3 cause the child to hate his room?

Not if you do it right. If the 1-2-3 is done correctly, it is simple and matter of fact. What may cause a child to hate his room, however, is all the yelling, name-calling, belittling, sarcasm, or hitting you may do if you don't use a method like this.

Does the room have to be a sterile environment?

No. Many books tell you the time out room should be modeled after a cell in a state penitentiary. This is unnecessary. The child can go to the room and read, take a nap, listen to the radio, play with legos, and so on. They don't even have to stay on their bed. Just to be safe, though, there are three things that are forbidden: no phone, no friends along, and no TV, Nintendo, or computer games.

Some people ask: "Well then, how does the 1-2-3 work? My kid just tells me that time out's fine with him—he doesn't care and he'll just go up and play." Don't pay much attention to any child who says, "I don't care." That comment usually means they do care. And if their room were such a great place to be, they would have already been up there. The fact of the matter is that the power of the 1-2-3 does not come so much from the time out itself; it comes from the interruption of the child's activities. No one— including you—likes to be interrupted.

Can you count different things to get to three?

Yes. In fact, you have to. It would drive you crazy if you had to have different counts for each type of misbehavior the youngster did. So if the child pushes his sister, "That's 1," throws a block across the room, "That's 2," and then (within 20 minutes) screams at you, "That's 3, take 5," and the child is gone.

Mom could say 1, Dad could say 2, and Mom or Dad could say, "That's 3." In fact, we encourage you to share the joy and spread it around some. Actually, it's better if Mom and Dad *do* do this, because then the kids know that both parents are behind the program, you are really serious, and it's easier for them to learn to shape up.

Can you ever ignore anything?

Yes, but don't do this in the beginning. *In the beginning, when in doubt, count!* After a while, when you're getting a good response at 1 or 2, you may be able to let up a little. Let's say, after getting used to the program, your child does something right in front of you that would normally be counted. Now the child can almost "feel" the count coming. Sometimes, if you say nothing, the child will spontaneously self-control and stop the misbehavior. This is ideal, because now the child is internalizing the rules.

How do you know when you should count? It's not too difficult to tell. Most of the time, if you're irritated about something and that something is a Stop behavior, you should be counting. Just to be sure, you can also write yourself a list (or do it with your spouse) of countable behavior and then show it to the kids.

What if we have other people over?

The other people who come over, for our purposes here, fall into three categories: other kids, other parents (with or without their kids), and, finally, grandparents.

Other kids. If your youngster has a friend over, count just as you would if no one else were there. If your child gets timed out, he goes to the room and—remember—his friend may not join him. Just explain to the other kid that you're using this weird system and his buddy will be back in five minutes or so. If your son or daughter says to you, as some have, "Dad, it's so embarrassing when you count me in front of my friends," you say to them once, "If you don't want to be embarrassed, you can behave."

Another thing you can do in this situation is count the other kid, too. It's your house. If his parent is there, though, you'd better ask their permission before you go disciplining their child.

Another variation, especially if you have a difficult child, is "1-2-3, 1-2-3, 1-2-3: out of the house to play." That means that at the third time out, instead of sending your child to the room again, both kids must now leave the house for a specified time (assuming the weather isn't brutal). Or 1-2-3, 1-2-3, 1-2-3, then send them over to the other kid's house to play for a while!

Other adults. If you have other people over to your house, get used to counting your child in front of them. It may feel a little funny at first, but it's a good idea to get used to it. Otherwise, it's quite easy for your children to sense that you are much easier prey when other parents are around.

What often happens, on the other hand, is something like this. You are together with another parent and their child. The two kids start goofing around and your child is doing something he shouldn't. You say, "That's 1," and he stops. The other parent looks at you like, "What did you do!?" So tell them about the 1-2-3 and explain how it works.

Grandparents. With regard to the 1-2-3, there are three types of grandparents, whether you're visiting them or they're visiting you. The first—and rarest—type of grandparent is the cooperative grandparent. They will count along with you. You say 1, Grandma says 2, and so on. But that doesn't happen a lot.

The second type of grandparent is the passive grandparent. They don't get involved, but they leave you alone and don't interfere either. That's fine.

The third type of grandparent is the antagonistic grandparent. They will say something to you like, "You had to read a book to learn how to raise your kids?! Why, when I was a girl, all daddy had to do was look at his belt...," and so on. Another kind of antagonistic grandparent will get in your way. You say to little Bobby, "That's 3, take 5," and before he moves Grandma butts in and says, "Oh, little Bobby didn't really do anything. Bobby, come and sit on Grandma's lap for a while."

Some parents ask at this point: "Can you count the grandparents?" Probably not, but you do have an assertiveness problem on your hands. You may have to say something like, "You know, Mom, I love you very much, but these are our kids and this is the way we're raising them. If you can't go along with the agenda, the visit may have to be cut short a little." Not easy to do, but important.

Can you imagine saying that to your parents!?

Can you use a time out chair instead of the room?

You can use a time out chair or couch, but only if the child does not goof around on it. Some kids, for example, sit on the chair at first, but eventually wind up off of it but just touching their little finger to it. They then look at you like "What are you going to do about this!?" This is too gamey and will ruin the discipline.

We usually prefer that visual contact between parent and child be broken during the rest period, so the child can't play games or provoke. Some parents, however, have already been successfully using chairs and many report that the kids sit still on them, don't talk too much, and don't keep getting off. That's fine.

There is also nothing sacred about the youngster's bedroom. Alternate rooms can be used that are more convenient, as long as they are reasonably safe.

What if the child won't go to his room?

If the child won't go to his room after you hit a count of three, remember that you are not allowed to use little adult attempts at persuasion, such as, "Come on now, do what Dad told you. It's only for five minutes and then you'll be able to go back and play—why can't you just do this one little thing for me?...etc, etc."

What you do instead depends on how big you are and how big the child is. Let's say you are 125 pounds, and your five year old son weighs 45. If he doesn't go to his room at 3, you simply move toward him. Some kids will then stay two feet ahead of you all the way to the room. That's OK. Others have to be "escorted," which can mean gently taking them by the arm, as well as dragging or carrying them. That's if you're 125 and they're 45.

Now let's imagine that it's five years later. Your ten year old now weighs 95 pounds, and you still weigh 125 (which would be good). You are no longer in a position to get into anything physical with this kid. He's too big, and wrestling matches make a fool out of you and out of your discipline. What you do instead is say, "That's 3, take 10, or it's a 10¢ fine. You pick." That means the youngster has a choice: a rest period or a fine.

What if he says, "Neither!" Then it's the fine, because you're in no position to wrestle him to his room. You say that ten cents doesn't mean anything to a ten year old these days? You might be right. Then double the fine, triple it, or convert it into lost TV minutes.

A problem emerges here, though, because the child hasn't gone to the room and isn't out of sight. Lots of kids in this situation are going to want to stay and argue with you about your stupid rules. You're not allowed to argue. Instead, you pull a "reverse time out," in which *you* exit the premises. Go to your room or the bathroom, stock them with good reading materials, and wait the storm out. Or walk around the house a few times. But don't talk.

What if the child won't stay in his room?

Many kids will stay in the room just fine, even if the door isn't shut (it doesn't have to be). Others, however, will keep coming out. One alternative is to just stand there or hold the door shut, but this won't work if you keep getting into major tugs of war on the door knob. Once again, if your discipline comes down to this, you are looking stupid and so are your methods.

Another alternative is to add minutes to the time out if the child comes out. This, of course, won't be much help with two or three year olds because they won't understand it, but with older children it can work well. Explain it once and then start doing it.

Some kids, however, are so rambunctious that they will just keep coming out and accumulate a million or so extra time out minutes. So what should you do? Put a lock on the door. This worries some parents, who think that their child will become claustrophobic. This hasn't happened yet, as far as we know, and you may not have to use the lock. What you do is tell the child that as long as he stays in the room, the door can remain open or unlocked. But the first time he comes out, the door gets locked for the rest period. Many children will quickly learn to stay put.

Many others, though, including some of our Attention Deficit (ADD) friends, will keep coming out no matter what you do, and locking them in is necessary. It is totally unproductive and harmful to have to be chasing them back in the room all the time, so the child must know that the door is a barrier that he's stuck with until the time is up.

What if the child won't come out?

You probably know the answer to this one: relax and enjoy yourself! Try not to cheat on extending the time out, though. Keep an eye on the clock or timer, then when the time is up tell the child and unlock the door (if necessary). If when you unlock the door, the youngster says, "I'm never coming out again as long as I live!", don't take the bait. Just walk away.

Some kids always want a hug and some reassurance when time out is over. What do you do? Give them a hug! If a child repeatedly requests a hug, however, you'd better check to make sure you're doing the 1-2-3 correctly. Does the child need this kind of reassurance because you were too harsh—emotionally or physically—before you sent them to the room?

How do you handle the *Horrors of the Telephone*?

This question brings back many memories to all parents. It seems that there are no parents in the entire world who have kids who don't act up when the parents are on the phone. Lots of kids start goofing around as soon as the thing rings, and often they are joined by the family pets!

What you do is count the children just as you would if you weren't on the phone. It's kind of like the earlier question about doing the 1-2-3 when you have other people over. You may have to interrupt the conversation to count. You may have to put the phone down or hang up before escorting a kid to their room. Long distance calls can become more expensive, but whatever it takes, do it. Otherwise the children will know that you are a sitting duck every time someone calls for you.

On a brighter note, some families get so good at doing the 1-2-3 that they don't say much anymore, they just hold up the appropriate number of fingers and the child responds. If you have gotten to this point, this is a handy tactic to use when you're talking on the telephone.

Doesn't it hurt the child's self-esteem, being counted all the time?

Many kids aren't counted very much, so that's no problem. Even for those who do get counted more often, however, if you are doing the 1-2-3 correctly, there should be no problem with hurting their self-esteem. In a way it's similar to the answer to the earlier question about their hating their rooms. What *will* hurt their self-esteem is all the yelling, arguing, name-calling, belittling, sarcasm, or hitting which you may do if you don't use a program like this. In addition, as you will see later, you can also balance off the counting (which is a kind of criticism) with "Sloppy PVF" (Positive Verbal Feedback).

What if the kid wrecks the room during his so-called "rest period"?

By far, the vast majority of children will not be room wreckers. This question is included, however, for two reasons. First of all, a small percentage of kids will kick holes in the wall, break things, and otherwise mess up the room, so some parents will need to know how to handle that. Second, the whole attitude of *1-2-3 Magic* is for parents to be ready for anything, rather than being defensive and thinking, "Oh no, what is he going to do now!?" Instead of that, we want your attitude and message to the children to be something like, "You're my child and I'm your parent. I love you, and it's my job to train and discipline you. I don't expect you to be perfect, and when you do do something wrong, here's what I'll do."

The credit for the solution to the room wrecking problem comes from a couple who were seen a long time ago. They had an eight year old boy who was very nice in the office, but "hell on wheels" everywhere else.

This couldn't go on, so Mom and Dad learned the 1-2-3 and went home to get started. This boy had been used to running the house. In fact, his parents kiddingly said they were thinking of putting his name on the mailbox! However, they were ready when they went home.

When the boy hit 3 for the first time, he couldn't believe it. How they got him to his room is still a mystery, but when he got there, he trashed the place. His first tactic—and perhaps the favorite of all room wreckers—was to empty his dresser and distribute his clothes all over the floor. Then he took the blankets and sheets off his bed and threw them around. Then the mattress and box springs were pushed off the bed frame. Next, he proceeded to his closet, took out all his hanging clothes, and threw them all over the room. Finally, he tore down his curtains.

What did his parents do? First of all, they didn't clean up the mess or have him clean it up. That would only have been loading his gun for the next time out: a perfectly neat room to wreck again. Second, they continued to count him aggressively. They didn't wimp out when he had a 2, and do fractions like, "That's 2.5, that's 2.7, that's 2.95, etc." They just hit him with the 3, and then sent him to the room to rearrange the trash. When bedtime came, he had to find his pajamas—and he had to find his bed. In the morning, his clothes for school didn't match for a week.

It took about ten days for him to calm down. After three days of peaceful time outs, they helped him clean up his room. After that— believe it or not—he hated to be counted, and he behaved very well at home and at school, where the teacher was also using the 1-2-3. Now he was the nice kid who had been seen in the office, and his parents were in charge at home as they should have been.

Two other things are important if you think you are going to have a room wrecker. If there is anything dangerous or harmful in the room, or there is anything valuable that can be broken, take it out before the first "rest period." If the child has a hammer and a saw in the room, or if Grandma has her Hummel collection on top of his dresser, for example, get those out of there before you start counting.

What if the kids count me back or count each other?

It doesn't count, so to speak. You're the only one who has the authority. If they are just teasing you when they count you back, ignore it. If they are really being nasty, count it.

Can't you ever talk to your kids?

When reading *1-2-3 Magic* some people get the impression that you're never supposed to talk to your children. This certainly isn't the case. The main idea is that you don't discuss things with a kid *when a rule is being enforced*. That just encourages testing. The rest of the time, however, you can talk your head off if you want to. In fact, after the 1-2-3 has been used for a while, there is usually a lot more time free for pleasant conversations. There is also a lot more time for affection and fun, since less time is wasted in useless arguing or yelling.

Also, think of it like this: discuss problems, but count attacks. If a child wants to talk something over with you, that's fine (see Chapter 20, Active Listening). It's also OK—up to a point—if they are frustrated and angry and are expressing that. But if their presentation degenerates into simply repeating themselves over and over, or into temper and verbal attacks on you, it should get counted (see Chapter 10, Testing and Manipulation).

Have we taken care of all possible questions? Not quite. The most commonly asked question needs a whole chapter devoted to it: *what do you do in public?*

Shouldn't the kids ever apologize?

If you're currently asking the kids to apologize, and you feel that's working well, fine. Keep in mind, however, that many apologies are really exercises in hypocrisy. A forced and quite begrudging "I'm sorry" from a child's mouth may embarrass them, but it may also be asking them to lie.

Should you ever spank a child?

There may be a time when a "spanking" is appropriate. For example, you have to physically escort a child to their room, and they physically attack you by kicking, hitting, scratching or biting. If a simple smack on the rear end—not full force and not repeated—helps them cooperate, fine.

However, one gruesome fact remains: *99% of all spankings are parental temper tantrums.* They are in no way attempts to train. They are simply the angry outburst of a parent who has lost control, doesn't know what to do, and who wants to hurt. Most parents who want to justify spanking kids are parents who have big problems with anger management. Remember, the whole point of the 1-2-3 program is to avoid the Talk-Persuade-Argue-Yell-Hit routine.

7

What to Do in Public

What to do in public is often the main worry of many parents after they have heard about how the 1-2-3 works. The first thing that comes to their minds is that there is no time out room. Don't worry. Believe it or not, that problem can be solved, and it's not the biggest problem you'll run into in public—by a longshot!

Your biggest problem in public is due to something else: the little devils can hold something over your head in public that they can't in private. *That something is the threat of public embarrassment!* No one wants to look like a child abuser in the candy section of the Piggly Wiggly grocery store. And these kids can pick up this fact, it appears, well before they are two years old.

So what are you going to do? The first thing you have to accept is that you will probably get burned in public more than in private. Studies of parents of hyperactive or ADD kids, for example, consistently show that these parents report they have their worst times when out of the house. The same may very well be true for all kids, but that certainly does not mean you are helpless. You have several options and they all can help a lot.

1. Don't Take Them Unless You Have To

Have you ever been to church on Sunday, and in the row ahead of you there is a couple with a two year old? The two year old isn't paying any attention to the service, and neither are his parents, since they are so preoccupied with trying to keep him in line. Around this trio are ten other people who also aren't paying any attention to the service, because they're busy evaluating how well the couple is disciplining their two year old.

So, in effect, we have thirteen people who might as well have not gone to church at all. Of course, we're not trying to talk you out of going to church, but think before you go anywhere, and don't ask for unnecessary trouble.

2. The Basic 1-2-3

There are plenty of times, naturally, when you must go out and you must take the kids. So imagine now that you are in the candy aisle, aisle 5, of the grocery store. Your five year old asks for a candy bar, you say "No," and—BOOM!—the kid has a major temper tantrum right there on the floor, complete with kicking, head banging, and yelling which can be heard out to the parking lot. What do you do?

You look down at the unhappy little monster, hold up one finger, and say, "That's 1." You say it as calmly and as firmly as you would at home, and you try your best not to be intimidated by the threat of public embarrassment and do something like saying "That's 1," and then sort of whispering, " Come on now, I don't want you making a fool of me in the candy section of the grocery store." You do that and the kid will *know* that you can be had for a nickel; he won't need the candy bar because he's about to have you for lunch.

Proceed to 2 and then to 3, if necessary. Many parents now wonder, what are we going to do at 3—there's no time out room here? It's true there's no time out room, but there are plenty of time out *places*. Over the years, we've collected the ideas of many creative parents who, in the heat of battle, were forced to come up with someplace for the rest period.

Here are a few of their ideas:

1. The grocery cart (for small children)

2. The corner of the store

3. The store's bathroom

4. Right where you stand—holding their hand

5. The car for a few minutes

6. If they're old enough, time them out of the store

During the time out, you do not talk to the child. No lecturing, screaming, or nagging. It's hard, but after a while the kids get the idea you mean business. And yes, there have been parents who felt the fuss was bad enough that they left a half full grocery cart and went home.

3. The '1-2-3-4'

Here's another idea. Tell the kids that you have to go shopping, it will take about an hour, and they have to go with you. You know they don't want to, but you're all stuck. But the deal is this: if they're "good" while you're out (meaning they don't hit a count of 3 or 4, depending on the length of the trip), you will buy them a treat at the end. This might be 50 to 75¢ worth of candy or whatever, provided they don't get the final count.

Some parents feel this is bribery. It is! But the real definition of bribery is paying someone to do something illegal. Here we're paying the kids to do something legal, and it works.

One family used this method when taking the kids out for a treat (ice cream) in the first place. The first time they tried it, the kids started their usual fighting in the back seat. Dad said, "That's 1, third time ends the trip." (A count of 3 was used because it was a short ride.) The kids then hit 2, and then 3. Dad turned the car around and drove back home. Several days later, the same thing happened: no one got any ice cream.

The next time they tried the ice cream trip, the kids must have finally believed Dad was serious. They hit a count of one, and then were good as gold the rest of the way.

4. Keep Moving

Another tactic that some parents have used successfully takes us back to our grocery store example with the youngster having a major fit in aisle 5, the candy section. What these parents have done is simply leave the child on the floor and move on to aisle 6. When they meet someone is aisle 6, they say, "Boy, do you hear all that racket over there?" Seriously, what often happens is that the child starts worrying where Mom or Dad went, forgets the candy, and runs to find them. Then again, some kids run to find their parent and then remember the candy and continue the tantrum. In that case you must return to the basic 1-2-3 mentioned above. If they *still* don't stop, you gut it out and finish your shopping, take them out to the car till they stop, or take them home.

Riding in the Car

Traveling in the car can present some extremely difficult situations to parents. Have you ever been riding along an interstate with your left hand on the wheel while your right hand is waving madly through the back seat trying to slap the kid who's just been teasing his sister for the 1000th time since you left the last town? This is not fun, and it can ruin vacations.

The car presents two problems: short trips and long trips. Here is what you can do:

Short trips

The basic 1-2-3 is very useful when chauffeuring the kids around town. The question is what to do at 3. One family didn't allow anyone to talk— including Mom and Dad—for fifteen minutes after the kids hit three. Other families have used fines (money taken off the allowance) usually at the rate of one or two cents for each minute that would have been included in the child's normal time out. A very effective tactic for many parents has been 1-2-3 and then pull the car off to the side of the road for the time out. It's rather dramatic and has quite an impact on the children.

Counting the kids in the car, and then having them serve the time outs when they get home isn't such a good idea, unless you're pretty close to home. The problem is that the rest period comes too long after the offense to do much good, and sometimes it just starts a fight as soon as you get home.

Long trips

Long trips with small children can be especially horrendous experiences unless parents are ready and know what to do. One of the biggest problems is usually sibling rivalry and all the fighting that goes with it. The car becomes more like a prison on wheels, and Mom and Dad are stuck in it.

One tactic that works well with small children is having the kids earn their spending money for the trip by not fighting. Why just give it to them without getting something—like peace and quiet—in return? The deal is this: for every fifteen minutes the children go without fighting, they each earn 10 to 25¢. *But there is a catch: they either both earn it, or they both lose it.* There is no time when one gets it and the other one doesn't. Take some paper and a timer with you in the car to keep an accurate accounting.

Other tactics that parents have used successfully have included the usual—and very helpful—things like the alphabet game and car bingo. Putting one child in the front and one in the back has been useful, as has been renting a VCR that plugs into the cigarette lighter or leaving at four in the morning so the kids sleep away the first part of the trip. Telling the kids they get 50¢ for every goat they see is also a brilliant maneuver.

The main point is this: don't ever leave on a long "vacation" with the kids without putting on your thinking cap first. Have the 1-2-3 and a few other tactics in your hip pocket, because you're going to need them.

Variations: Sibling Rivalry, Tantrums & Pouting

There are three problems that kids present that require some minor modifications in the 1-2-3. These are sibling rivalry, temper tantrums, and pouting.

Sibling Rivalry

The difficulty here is that now you have more than one child acting up, so how are you going to handle this? There are several important rules that you should follow.

1. *Count both kids.* When the children are fighting, you should count both of them 90% of the time or so. Why? Because kids are tricky, and it is often very hard to tell who started it—even if you are right there. Have you ever been driving in the car with the kids in the back seat and you hear, "Mom, he's looking at me again!"? Who started that one? There's no way to tell. So you count both children, unless one is the obvious, unprovoked aggressor. But be careful.

2. *Never ask the world's stupidest question.* Every parent knows what that is: "What happened?" or "Who started it?" What do you expect

to hear? All you get is the kids blaming one another and yelling a lot. The only time you really need to ask anything is if you think someone might be physically injured.

3. *Don't expect an older child to act more mature during a fight.* It doesn't even matter if they're eleven and four years old. Don't say to the eleven year old, "She's only a baby, can't you put up with a little teasing once in a while?" That's loading the gun of the four year old, and they'll be sure to take advantage of it.

This is a little off the subject, but imagine for a second that that eleven year old comes up to you later and says, "I want to ask you a question."

"Go ahead," you say.

"How come I always get a ten minute time out, and Miss Shrimp there only has to go for five minutes?" he continues.

"Because the rule in our house," you say, "is one minute of time out for each year of your life."

"Well that's the dumbest thing I ever heard of!" he yells.

"That's 1."

This child doesn't want to talk and he doesn't really want information. He wants a fight and you're not going to get sidetracked into a useless argument.

What if the kids have a fight and they share the same room? It's not a real brilliant idea to send two fighting children to the same room. Send one to their room and the other to an alternate time out room. Then for the next rest period reverse the places. If they fight on the way to the rooms, extend the time outs by five or ten minutes.

Temper Tantrums

The problem with a temper tantrum is simple: what if the time out is up and the child's not done with the tantrum? The answer: the time out doesn't start until the tantrum is over. So if it takes the youngster fifteen minutes to calm down, the rest period starts after fifteen minutes or so. And if it takes the kid two hours to calm down, the time out starts after two hours. You also are not allowed to stick your head in the room every ten minutes and tell the child to quiet down. Just leave them alone.

The only children we don't use the temper tantrum variation for are the two and three year olds. They don't seem to get it, so just let them out after a couple of minutes and see what happens. If they still don't quiet down, then leave them in longer.

Pouting

The trouble with pouting is that it is a very passive behavior and it's designed to make you feel guilty. If you do wind up feeling guilty, that's really more your problem. Why should you feel bad for doing what you're supposed to do as a parent? You shouldn't.

So if you discipline a child and they give you the martyr look, just turn around and walk away. The only time you would do something different is if you get what we call an "aggressive pouter." That's a child who follows you all over the place to make sure you don't miss a minute of the sour face. If they do that, "That's 1."

Getting Started:
The Kickoff Conversation

Getting started with the 1-2-3 is pretty easy, but don't put a lot of stock in the impact your initial conversation with the kids will have. Plenty of children don't really get the idea until you've been counting for a while, and after they've been to their rooms a few times.

So, even though it's a little bit too much like little adult stuff, give the kids the benefit of the doubt and tell them what you'll be doing. If both parents are living at home, Mom and Dad sit down with the kids in the two to twelve year range and say something like this:

"Listen, you guys know there are times when you do things we don't like. From now on we're going to do something a little different. When we see you doing something you're not supposed to, we'll say, 'That's 1.' That's like a warning and it means you're supposed to stop. If you don't stop, we'll say, 'That's 2.' If you still don't stop, we'll say, 'That's 3, take 5 (or however many minutes for your age).' That means you have to go to your room for a time out or a kind of rest period. When you come out, we don't talk about what happened unless it's really necessary. We just forget it and start over.

"If the thing you're doing is real bad to start with, like swearing at us or hitting, we'll say, 'That's 3, take 10 or 15.' That means there aren't any warnings except that one, and you just go straight to your room. Do you have any questions?"

Expect the kids to sit there and look at you like you've gone off your rocker. Some kids will poke each other and exchange knowing glances, as if to say, "Well, it looks like Mom went to the library again and got another one of those books on how to raise us guys. Last time she stuck to it for about a week. I think if we stick together and hang tough, we should be running the house again inside of two weeks, right?"

Wrong. Don't expect them to be grateful or to look enlightened. Just stick to your guns, get going, and, when in doubt, count!

At this point of this book, you may feel that you're ready to start using the 1-2-3, but not so fast! If you began counting right now, you wouldn't be prepared for the fact that many children—about half—are not going to thank you for your efforts. Instead, they are going to engage in one or more of the Six Kinds of Testing and Manipulation. You've got to know what these are and how to handle them before you get going.

Part III:

No Child Will Thank You

10

The Six Kinds of Testing & Manipulation

Up to this point, you are almost—but not quite—ready to start using the 1-2-3 for Stop behavior problems with your children. The reason you're not totally ready yet has to do with the fact that the kids will not thank you for your efforts to discipline them more effectively and make your house a happier place in which to live. In fact, as mentioned earlier, many children will test you immediately. They will get worse before they get better.

So you have to be ready for *Testing and Manipulation (T & M)*. These are the efforts of the frustrated child to weasel their way out of something, avoid the discipline, or sidetrack you in your efforts. Several things need to be remembered about testing and manipulation.

1. *Testing occurs when the child is frustrated.* You are not giving him what he wants; you are counting him; you are making him do homework or go to bed. He doesn't like this and hopes for a way out.

2. *Testing, therefore, is purposeful behavior.* The purpose of testing and manipulation, obviously, is for the child to get his way, rather than allowing you to impose your will on him. Actually, T&M can have two purposes, which may come in sequence.

A. The first purpose of testing and manipulation is for the child to get what he wants.

B. The second purpose of T&M kicks in if the first fails: if the child cannot get his way, he will get something else: *REVENGE*.

---

3. *When using T&M, the child has a "choice" of six possible tactics.* All six can serve the first purpose; five of the six can serve the second purpose.

Just about all parents and teachers recognize all these tactics. They have seen them many times. They also usually know which ones are used by which children. They may also recognize some of their own favorites, because adults use the same basic T&M methods as kids.

Here are the six tactics that frustrated children use on their adult tormentors:

1. Badgering

Badgering is like the "Please, please, please," or "Why, why, why?" business. The child just keeps after you and after you and after you, trying to wear you down with repetition. "Just give me what I want and I'll shut up!" is kind of the idea of the whole procedure. And kids can be amazingly persistent.

If the parent attempts to verbally respond to everything the child says and every time he says it, Mom or Dad is in for a very long and frustrating evening. Many parents continue on a long, wild goose chase looking for the right words or reasons that will make the kid be quiet.

2. Intimidation

Intimidation is an aggressive attack, and often involves temper tantrums. Here the aggravated child may yell at you, accuse you of being a bad parent, or otherwise storm around the house. Older kids sometimes get into swearing. Younger children may throw themselves on the floor, bang their heads, and kick around ferociously.

3. Threat

"I'll never speak to you again!"
"I'm going to kill myself!"
"I'm not eating dinner and I won't do my homework!!"
"I'm going to kill the parakeet!"
"I'm running away from home!"

These are all examples of threats. Something bad is going to happen to you unless you cease and desist from this ridiculous discipline at once.

4. Martyrdom

Actually not talking, not eating dinner, or sitting in the closet for two hours might be examples of martyrdom.

"No one around here loves me anymore. Might as well find another family to live with."

Crying, pouting, and looking sad or teary can also be effective. Here the goal, obviously, is to get the parent feeling guilty, and Martyrdom is surprisingly effective against lots and lots of parents. It seems that many Moms and Dads have a "guilt button" the size of the state of Wyoming! All the kids have to do is push it, and then *they* run the house.

The first four tactics, Badgering, Intimidation, Threat, and Martyrdom, share a common, underlying dynamic. The child, in a sense—and without quite knowing what he's doing, is saying to the parent something like, "Look, you're making me uncomfortable by not giving me what I want. Now I'm making you uncomfortable with all this harping at you, temper tantrums, ominous statements, and feeling sorry for myself. *Now that we're both uncomfortable, I'll make you a deal: you call off your dogs and I'll call off mine."*

Sounds good, right? If you do give in, you are almost guaranteed that the T&M will stop immediately. The problem, however, is then who's running your house? It certainly isn't you, it's the kids. All they have to do in a difficult situation is get out their big guns and they've got you.

5. Butter Up

The fifth tactic takes a different tack. Instead of making you feel uncomfortable, the child tries to make you feel good.

"Gee, Mom, you've got the prettiest eyes of anybody on the block."

Or, "I think I'll go clean my room. It's been looking kind of messy for the last three weeks. And after that maybe I'll take a look at the garage."

Here something good is going to happen, and this kind of testing sometimes precedes the frustrating event. Have you ever heard a parent say, "The only time he's ever good is when he wants something." That's probably Butter Up, or what is also called "Sweetness and Light." This type of manipulation is occasionally kind of tricky, because it's hard to tell apart from genuine affection.

6. Physical

This is perhaps the worst. Here the frustrated child either physically attacks you, breaks things, or runs away. Children don't usually start doing this all of a sudden. Many of them have a long history of this kind of behavior, and the bigger they get, the scarier it gets.

We took a brief survey once of parents, and later of teachers, and asked them which tactics they thought the children used the most. Interestingly, both groups mentioned the same three: Badgering, Intimidation, and Martyrdom.

And the favorite was Martyrdom.

The $64,000 Question

Now comes the big question. Think of your kids, one at a time, and ask yourself, "Does this child have one—or perhaps two—tactics that they use very frequently or even all the time?" If the answer is yes, this is probably bad. Why? Because the tactic probably works. People tend to repeat something because it works for them.

What does "it works" mean?

It goes back to the two purposes of testing and manipulation. First of all, the child may be successfully getting his way by using the tactic.

How do you know if a child is getting his way by testing? It's obvious—you just give it to him. You turn back on the TV, stop counting, or don't make him do his homework or go to bed.

"It works" can also refer to the second purpose of T&M: *Revenge.* How do you know if a child is effectively getting revenge? It goes back to the No-Talking, No-Emotion Rules. If this child can get you all upset, or get you talking too much, they know they've got you. You are uncomfortable and paying for your sins. Let's say you want the homework done, and the child pulls #2 on you, Intimidation. Yelling, screaming, banging things—the whole nine yards. Your response, however, is a *counter* temper tantrum. Final score: Child 5, Parent 2. They've got you: the small, inferior part of the youngster got the big splash from the larger, "more powerful" adult.

Or say your child does a #4 (Martyrdom): "Well, it's obvious that nobody around here loves me anymore. I might as well hitch the next freight to Iowa (touch of #3, Threat)." You feel frightened, guilty. You are certain that unloved children grow up to be homeless people or serial killers.

You sit the youngster down on your lap, and for a half hour tell him how much you love him, how much Dad and the dog love him, etc., etc. You have just been had by tactic #4, Martyrdom. Unless you are a grossly neglectful or abusive parent, your kids know that you love them, and you should tell them that you love them.

But you never tell them that you love them when they're pulling a #4 on you, Martyrdom.

Doing It Right

Now, let's say you're learning the 1-2-3 and you're toughening up a bit. Your ten year old child wants to go to a friend's house at 9 PM on a school night. You say no, and the following scene occurs:

"Why not? Come on, just this once!" (Badgering)
"Can't do it."

"You never give me anything around here!" (Martyrdom)

"I don't think you're too underprivileged."

"I promise I'll clean the garage later." (Butter Up)

"The garage is OK now. I just did it."

"This stinks—I HATE YOUR GUTS!" (Intimidation)

"Sorry."

The child tries to hit you on the arm. (Physical)

"Watch your step, pal."

"Oh, please, PLEASE, oh, come on, it's not so late." (Badgering)

"No way, Jose—it's outa bounds for you."

"If you don't, I'm gonna split for good." (Threat)

This is no fun, but something constructive is happening. The child is fishing around, switching tactics, and probing for your weak spot. He can't find it. You are sticking to your guns, and remaining fairly calm in spite of the aggravation.

The only thing wrong with this example has to do with how you should handle testing and manipulation. You would not let the child switch tactics that many times. Why? Because if you look at the original six T&M tactics, five of them are Stop behaviors (except for Butter Up). So if a child were pushing you this much, you would count him.

Remember the twinkie example? This is how it should be handled:

"Yeah, but I want one." (Badgering)

"That's 1."

"You never give me anything!" (Martyrdom)

"That's 2."

"This is so stupid! I'm going to kill myself and then run away from home!!" ("23" pattern: Intimidation plus Threat)

"That's 3, take 5."

What to Expect

We mentioned before that the kids would fall basically into two categories when you start the 1-2-3: immediate cooperators and immediate testers. You just enjoy the immediate cooperators.

The immediate testers will get worse at first. When you try to take away the power of their former favorite T&M method, they will initially respond in one of two ways. They will *"up the ante"* for a particular tactic, making it much worse. The volume and length of a tantrum, for example, may double. Their other response will be to *switch tactics*, perhaps trying some new ones or others they haven't used for years. Tactic switching is aggravating, but remember that it is almost always a sign that you are doing well in being firm.

Keep your mouth shut. Count when necessary. Eventually tactic escalation and tactic switching will diminish, and the result will be that the youngster begins to accept your discipline without having a major cow every time. You then have won the battle. You are the parent; they are the children, and your home is a more peaceful place.

Some kids, after doing well for a while, later become sort of "delayed testers." This can come when the novelty of the new system wears off, they begin to realize that they aren't getting their way anymore, or your routine gets disrupted by travel, visitors, illness, new babies or just plain time.

Delayed testing can be somewhat disillusioning, because "the kids were so good before!" You may feel like the whole system is falling apart. Or that it was too good to be true and too nice to last.

But really, all you need to do is read over the book again, discuss it with your spouse if possible, then get back to basics: No-Talking, No-Emotion, be gentle but aggressive, when in doubt count, take it to them nicely...and things should shape up fairly quickly.

The 1-2-3 is easy to come back to.

11

Counting in Action

H ere are some examples of the 1-2-3 in action, with brief commentary on how well Mom, Dad, or teacher did in handling the situation.

General Stop Behavior

Mark, three years old, is picking up an old cigarette butt from the ash tray and looking at it quizzically.

"No, Mark, put that down."
Mark picks up another one.
"Mark, that's 1."
Mark just stands there, holding the cigarettes.
"That's 2."
Mark drops the cigarettes.

Comment: Good job, short and sweet. It's much easier for the toddler to focus on and understand the crisp instruction. "Come one now, honey, that's yukky and you'll get your hands all dirty..." is more confusing and offers the alternative of testing.

Requests

Eight year old Tom asks his mother if he can use his Dad's electric jig saw.

> "I don't think so. You better wait till Daddy's home."
> "Oh come on, Mom. I know how to do it."
> "No, I think it's too dangerous."
> "There's nothing else to do." (Badgering, Martyrdom)
> "I said no. That's 1."
> "THAT'S 1! THAT'S 2! THAT'S 3! THAT'S 12! THAT'S
> 20! THAT'S STUPID!" (Intimidation)
> "That's 2."
> "Didn't know you could count that high." (Intimidation)
> "That's 3, take 10 and add 5 for the mouth."
> "Gee, I'll need a calculator for this one."

Mom moves toward Tom to escort him if necessary, but he goes to his bedroom.

<u>Comment</u>: One explanation and then count. Mom also adds five for the smart mouth, and she has the presence of mind to stay cool in spite of the insult. When her son doesn't go to the rest period right away, she also does not get caught up in a stupid argument or other little adult conversations.

Interrupting

Mom and Dad are having an important and private conversation on the couch. Seven year old Michelle jumps in between.

> "Hi, guys!"
> "Hi, honey. Listen, Mom and Dad have to talk about something
> very important for a few minutes, so you go play for a little
> bit."
> "I wanna be here with you. I promise I won't listen."
> "No, dear. Come on now, you go and play."
> "I don't have anything to do." (Badgering)
> "Listen, young lady. We're not going to tell you again!"
> "THERE'S NOTHING ELSE FOR ME TO DO!" (Intimidation)

"Do you want a spanking!?"
Michelle starts crying. (Martyrdom)
"OK, that's 1."
Michelle leaves, crying.

Comment: Pretty sloppy job by Mom and Dad. They only get around to counting after ridiculous attempts at persuasion, threatening a spanking, and risking World War III for nothing. They eventually recover and count.

Arguing

Eleven year old Jeff asks:

"Can I go out after dinner to play?"
"No, dear, you still have homework to do," says Mom.
"I'll do it when I come back in, right before bed."
"That's what you said last night, honey, and it didn't work. Remember?"
"Oh, please Mom. I promise!" (Badgering, Butter Up)
"Get your homework done first, and then you can go out. If you work hard, it shouldn't take more than a half hour."
"Why can't I just go out now!? I'll DO MY STUPID HOME WORK!" (Intimidation)
"That's 1."
"I can't wait to grow up so I can go in the Army. It's got to be more fun than living in this dump." (Martyrdom)
"That's 2."
"All right, all right, all right." Jeff goes to start his homework.

Comment: Mom did very well here. She tried a little negotiating, but when that didn't work she didn't get caught up in a stupid argument or try to explain why her house wasn't the same as the military.

Classroom Misbehavior

Margaret is attempting to write her assignment on a piece of paper, but she is using orange chalk. Her teacher, Mrs. Simpson, notices and suggests a different approach.

"Margaret, the assignment can't be done with orange chalk."

"Why not?"

"Don't you have a pen or a pencil?"

"What's wrong with chalk?"

"You know what's wrong with chalk. You know better than that."

"I think it looks OK."

"Listen, I'm not going to tell you again. It's not acceptable like that."

"I can read it."

"That's 1."

"Oh, for pete's sake!" (Margaret gets out a pen)

Comment: Mrs. Simpson gets into too much talking in the beginning in an obviously ridiculous situation, but then catches herself.

Sibling Rivalry I

Nine year old John and his seven year old sister Suzie are best of friends and best of enemies. They are playing with legos on the living room floor. Dad is watching the football game on TV and so far is amazed they are getting along so well, but the fun is about to end.

"Suzie, I need another wheel for my tank," says John inquiringly.

"No, John, I've got it on my wagon," says Suzie nervously.

Dad squirms a bit in his chair. It's fourth and goal for the good guys.

"Lemme just use one wheel now. I'll give it back to you later," suggests brother.

"No, my wagon needs four wheels," replies sister.

"Your wagon looks stupid!"

"Dad, John's gonna take one of my wheels and I had them first!"

The good guys had to try for a field goal and it was blocked. Dad is not pleased.

"Both of you, knock it off!"

"She doesn't need to hog all the wheels. There aren't enough

for me to make what I want, and they're my legos."
"But I made this first!"
"OK, kids, that's 1 for both of you."
"She's an idiot." John smashes his creation and leaves.

Comment: Not bad. Perhaps Dad should have counted sooner instead of saying "Knock it off!" Should Dad have counted John for smashing his tank or badmouthing his sister? Some parents would count this, but others wouldn't because the tank was his (and it can be rebuilt) and John is perhaps using a constructive tactic in leaving the situation.

Dog Teasing

Four year old Michael has the dog backed into a corner and pushed up against the wall. The dog, normally patient, is starting to snarl. Mom intervenes.

"Michael, don't tease the dog, honey."
Michael giggles but continues pushing the dog up the wall.
"That's 1."
"No! I wanna pet him." Dog snarls again.
"That's 2."
"I WANNA PET HIM!" (Intimidation) Continues torturing.
"That's 3. Upstairs."
Michael falls on floor, releasing the dog, but yelling and crying.
Mom drags the unwilling body to the bedroom for time out.

Comment: Couldn't have done it better. No talking while "escorting" the child to the rest period.

Potential Spontaneous Sleepovers

"Can I have a friend sleep over tonight?"
"I don't think so, it's already eight thirty."
"You let Jimmy have someone last night."
"That was because he asked a week ago."
"Come on, Mom, it's not too late." (Badgering)

"No, dear. Not this time."

"We'll be real quiet and won't stay up late." (Badgering, Butter Up)

"I never get to do anything." (Martyrdom)

"You never get to do anything? Oh, really? Where did I take you today? Tell me."

"That wasn't any fun anyway!" (Indimidation, Martyrdom)

"Well apparently nothing I do is good enough for you, young lady."

"ALL I WANT IS TO HAVE JULIE SLEEP OVER!"

"YOU LISTEN TO ME! I'M SICK OF THIS!" Etc., etc., etc.

<u>Comment</u>: Super bad news. Did the child's Martyrdom push the guilt button and then trigger an angry overreaction?

Sibling Rivalry II

Sean (9) and Tammi (11) are getting into it while trying to play Scrabble in the living room. Dad is washing dishes in the kitchen.

"It's my turn."

"No it isn't. You lost it cause you took so long."

"Give me that. I was going to pick up that one!"

"You scratched me!"

"I did not, you idiot! You started it!"

"You're so dumb it isn't funny."

Dad enters. "What's going on here?"

"She's cheating!"

"I am not, lamebrain, you're too slow!"

"Be quiet, both of you! Tell me what happened."

General yelling and chaos follow the ill fated inquiry.

"OK, that's 1 for both of you."

General yelling and chaos continue.

"That's 2."

Sean dumps the Scrabble board over, grabs a bunch of letters and throws them at the piano.

"Sean, that's 3, take a rest for 10."

<u>Comment</u>: Dad recovered pretty well after asking the world's dumbest question.

Summertime Boredom

It's only August 3rd, and school is still three weeks off. It's hot. Three kids at home today. Mom doesn't know how long she'll last. Jimmy starts the whining first.

"There's nothing to do."

"Why don't you guys go down to the pool?"

"We just went there yesterday. And it's too hot."

"Why don't you play that new Nintendo game?"

"Nah."

"Why don't you walk to Alaska?"

"What?"

"Just kidding." Mom laughs.

"Mom, it's not funny!"

"Well, don't go giving me a hard time about it. Everything I
    suggest isn't good enough for your highness. I'm not the
    entertainment committee around here, so find something
    yourself and leave me alone!"

"You said you'd take us to Creature Castle at the new mall."

"Well, I can't today. I have too many things to do around here."

"See, we never get to do anything we want!"

<u>Comment</u>: Nice conversation if you're into self-torture. Counting should have been used early on here. What is Mom expecting the child to say, "Thanks for the suggestions."?

Talking in Class

Sally and Marci start a conversation across the aisle during geography. Mrs. Smith interrupts her discussion of crops in Brazil.

"Girls, I need your attention."

"The girls stop talking for thirty seconds, but then can't resist
    finishing what they started.

"Sally, Marci, that's 1."

The girls stop talking.

Comment: Crisp and to the point. Easier on the children's self-esteem than a lot of righteous criticism.

Part IV:

Encouraging Good Behavior

12

The Six Start
Behavior Tactics

We will now turn our attention to managing Start behavior—
the positive things you want to encourage the children to do. This
category includes things like doing schoolwork, going to bed, eating,
cleaning rooms, practicing musical instruments, and getting up and out in
the morning.

*It's a good idea, when beginning this program, to use the 1-2-3 first
for a week to ten days or so before worrying about Start behavior.* It's a
little too complicated and too much to keep straight if you try to do the
whole program at once. It will also be considerably easier to get the kids
to do the good things if you have first gotten back in control of the house.

You will also need to use the 1-2-3 to handle testing and manipulation,
which is also going to occur when you are using your Start behavior
tactics. Remember that the kids are not going to thank you for doing any
of this. Since testing is a Stop behavior, if you work on counting negative
behavior first, you will have had a fair amount of experience in dealing
with it before you tackle the task of getting the kids to do the good things
you want them to.

There are six Start behavior tactics you can consider using, and these will be described in just a second. It is important, however, to first keep in mind several general rules:

A. *You can always try a Simple Request first* (just as you can with Stop behavior). Ask the child to clean his room or tell them it's time to start practicing the clarinet. If they don't respond, though, don't get caught up in attempts at persuasion using Little Adult ideas.

B. *Start behavior tactics can often be combined.* You don't have to use just one for each type of problem, and you can be somewhat creative.

C. *Angry people make noise; happy ones do not.* We all suffer from a biological curse that motivates us to say something to our kids when we're angry. Then we tend to keep quiet when we're feeling things are going OK. The result is not good. Other family members can start feeling they're just a pain in the neck if we don't regularly try to hand out some reinforcing or appreciative comments. The first Start behavior strategy (Sloppy PVF) is a good antidote for this curse.

D. *Train them or be quiet!* In the 1-2-3 program there is a method or way of handling just about all the kinds of problems your kids can throw at you. So use them! If the child isn't cleaning his room, train him to clean it. Otherwise, be quiet, clean it yourself, or close the door and don't look. *Training, however, does not mean nagging, arguing, yelling, or hitting.*

With this in mind, let's take a look at the six tactics you will use to get the kids to do what they're supposed to.

Sloppy PVF

Sloppy Positive Verbal Feedback, otherwise known as praise or reinforcement, should be dished out on a regular basis. Like voting in Chicago, Sloppy PVF should be done early and often. If you look, you shouldn't have trouble finding something to reinforce. Or once you've gotten the kids going with some other Start behavior tactic, positive reinforcement can help keep it going. The "sloppy" refers to the fact that you don't reinforce everything all the time. In fact, some irregularity to your praise is probably a good idea.

Here are some examples of Sloppy PVF:

"Thanks for doing the dishes."

"You started your homework all by yourself!"

"You kids did a good job of getting along during the movie."

"I think you got ready for school in record time this morning!"

"Good job on that math test, John."

"That's wonderful! I can't believe it! How on earth did you do that!?"

Sloppy PVF should be "tailored" to the child. Some kids like rather elaborate, emotional verbal reinforcement, like the last example above. Other kids are embarrassed by it, and may prefer statements like the second to the last example. Pay attention to your child's reactions to see if you can tell what they prefer.

How do you keep it up on a regular basis? As mentioned before, this is surprisingly quite difficult, since most of us tend to shut up when we are content. Here are two thoughts. First, see if you can dish out two positive comments for every one negative comment. This doesn't have to be done right at the same time, of course, but it can be done later. If that idea doesn't appeal to you, a second strategy is to do a quota system: each day you make a deal with yourself that you will make at least five positive comments to each child (you might want to consider doing the same with your spouse!).

Kitchen Timers

Kitchen timers are great helps for lots of Start behaviors, such as homework, getting up in the morning, eating, and going to bed. They can also be used to time the time outs themselves. You can even take them in the car with you. Kids, especially the younger they are, have a natural tendency to want to beat the things.

You could say to a five year old, for example, "You've got three things in the kitchen I would like picked up and put in your room. I'm setting the timer for ten minutes and I'll bet you can't beat it!"

The response will often be, "Oh yes I can!", and the youngster will be off. You could also do this with an eleven year old, but you would phrase it in a more matter of fact manner. If the child doesn't respond by picking up the things, you can later use the Docking System.

Kitchen timers are also helpful because they are not testable, i.e., they don't respond when a child uses one or more of the T&M tactics, such as Badgering or Intimidation or Martyrdom.

The Docking System

The idea of the Docking System is like docking wages: if you don't do the work, you don't get paid. This, of course, requires that the kids have an allowance, and you could consider starting this with children five or older. The allowance doesn't have to be anything large, but it's a good idea to have half of it based on doing things around the house (e.g., cleaning their room, chores, homework). The other is simply given to the child, partly so you are sure you have some leverage when it comes time to use the Docking procedure.

What do you do then? Let's imagine you've been having the typical parent-child discussion about getting a dog. The child wants the dog, but you wisely object that they probably won't take care of it on their own. Let's assume you get the dog (because you want one too).

What do you do? You tell the child what the deal will be. He's eleven and gets about $3 per week allowance. You want the dog fed by six o'clock each night. If he feeds the dog by then, fine (use Sloppy PVF). If he doesn't get to the dog by six, you have good news and bad news. The good news is that you will feed the dog. The bad news is that you charge to feed other people's dogs, and for this mutt it will be fifteen cents per feeding taken off the $3 allowance. The child agrees.

Here's how it might go. The first night it's ten after six, there's no child around, and the dog's looking hungry. You wait. At quarter after your son comes running in asking if you fed the dog. You say, "No." He says, "Good!" and feeds the dog. You give him some Sloppy PVF—he was only a little bit late.

The second night it's twenty after six and you finally feed the dog. At six-thirty the boy comes running in:

"Did you feed the dog?"
"Yes, I did, and I had to charge you fifteen cents off your allowance."
"WELL, WHAT DID YOU DO THAT FOR!?" (Yelling)

"That's 1."

This is not going to be a discussion. It's simply one version of testing tactic # 2, Intimidation, and it should be counted. In this kind of situation, it's extremely difficult to resist the temptation to get into little adult types of comments, such as, "Do you remember when we bought this stupid mutt for you? What did you say, huh? You said, 'I'll feed the dog every single night. No problem!' Right! Well, here we are on only the second night and I'm already feeding your dog! I'm sick of doing everything around here and you kids are going to have to learn..."

What you're saying may be absolutely correct, but it will do no good and cause some harm. Be quiet and let the money do the talking. If money doesn't seem to have much clout with the child, take minutes off their TV time.

Natural Consequences

Here you let the big, bad world teach the child what works and what doesn't. There are times when staying out of some problems is the best thing. Suppose you have a fourth grader who is taking piano lessons for the first time. She is not practicing like she should, however, and then every night is up worrying about her piano teacher being mad at her.

What should you do? Nothing. Some piano teachers are very good at getting uncooperative kids to tickle the ivories on a regular basis between lessons. If after a few weeks, this doesn't work, you may want to try other Start behavior tactics, such as using the timer or charting. But leave it alone for a while in the beginning.

Or, suppose you have a sixth grader. He's supposed to make his own lunch, with stuff that you buy, and then brown bag it to school. It seems like every day he is yelling at you about how hungry he was at lunch with nothing to eat. What should you do? Relax, and give him some encouragement by saying something like, "I'm sure you'll do better tomorrow." If his Badgering continues, it should be counted.

Another example of a good time to use natural consequences? Wintertime dress. All parents know that junior high and high school students think there are federal laws against zipping or buttoning up their coats in the winter. Let them feel a little cold if they're not dressed properly, and avoid the obvious lecture.

Charting

Charting involves using something like a calendar which you can put on the refrigerator door, or on the back of the child's bedroom door. You have the days of the week across the top, and down the side each row represents a different task the child is working on, such as cleaning their room, getting to bed, and feeding the dog. If the child completes the task to your satisfaction, you indicate this on the chart with stickers for the little kids (3 to 8) and grades or numbers (A-F, 5-1) for the older children.

Here's what a chart might look like. This child is working on cleaning his room, brushing his teeth, and feeding the dog:

	Sun	Mon	Tues	Wed	Thurs	Fri	Sat
Room							
Teeth							
Dog							

Reinforcement with charting comes, hopefully, from two things: parental praise (Sloppy PVF) and the inherent satisfaction from doing a good job. These often work well to stimulate a child to do the job. However, sometimes they just don't work. Your child is just a natural slob and a clean room means nothing to him. Or your little girl is ADD and LD, and homework provides very little or no satisfaction for her.

Here you must go with artificial reinforcers—sometimes referred to as bribery. This is OK, and some kids need something pleasant in order to help them overcome their aversion or indifference to the project. Reinforcers can be part of one's allowance, or special meals, or baseball cards, or staying up later at night occasionally. The best ideas are relatively small things that can be dished out in small pieces and frequently. Try to be as creative as possible in coming up with reinforcers. They certainly do not have to always be material. Some kids, for example, will work hard to earn minutes to stay up later at night, or to be able to do some special activity with one of their parents.

Keep the chart simple. Three or four things to work on at one time is enough; more gets too confusing. Also, build in "discontinuation criteria"—rules to use for when it is time to not use the chart anymore. You certainly are not going to do charting forever, and too often its effects can fade primarily because Mom and Dad are simply getting tired of doing it. You might say, for example, that if the child gets good (defined precisely) scores for two weeks running, that item will be taken off the chart. When the child has earned their way off the chart entirely, it's time to go out for pizza and a movie to celebrate. If the child regresses, you can reinstate the chart.

The 1-2-3 (different version)

This may seem kind of odd, but the 1-2-3, which was earlier used for Stop behavior, can also be used for Start behavior, but only on one condition: what you want the child to do cannot take over two minutes. So if the child throws their coat on the floor after school, and you ask them to pick it up and they don't, just say, "That's 1." If they get timed out, they go and serve the time, and when they come out, you ask them to pick it up again. If no cooperation, another time out follows. Keep this up until they get the idea.

What if they are just in a totally ornery mood and never get the idea? Just switch to the Docking System. You hang up the coat for them, but you charge for your services. Keep the talking to a minimum, and count whining, arguing, yelling and other forms of hassling (T&M).

What can you use this version of the 1-2-3 for? Things like feeding the dog, brushing teeth, or just, "Would you please come here for a second?" might take less than two minutes. What can you not use the 1-2-3 for? Obviously, longer projects like homework, eating dinner, getting up and out in the morning, and so on.

When working on encouraging positive behavior, remember the rule that says, "Train them or be quiet." Also, be careful with what we call "spontaneous requests." Spontaneous requests are requests that parents make of their children sort of on the spur of the moment—when the parent sees that the room is messy, or the clothes are still in the dryer, they ask their youngster—who is watching TV—to take care of the problem. The child reacts with hostility and then the parents says, "Why can't you do just this one little thing for me when we do everything all the time for you? What's the big deal? Now MOVE!"

In a way, parents are correct here, but they're also being very naive. No kid likes being interrupted. Spontaneous requests certainly can't be avoided, but *they always maximize irritability and minimize cooperation.* When asked to do something, is the child supposed to say, "Thanks for giving me this unanticipated opportunity to be of service."?

Not likely. Try to minimize spontaneous requests and maximize use of the six start behavior tactics.

Up and Out
in the Morning

C lose to the top of the list for greatest Start behavior hassles is the problem of getting the kids up and out of the house in the morning. This is a problem for older kids who are school age mostly, though it can apply to preschoolers too. This situation often brings out the worst in everybody. Many people—parents and kids—are naturally crabby in the morning and there is the pressure of having to get someplace *on time*. The nervousness, nagging and emotional thunderstorms that result can easily ruin a parent's day.

For the kids, getting up and out in the morning involves a whole sequence of Start behaviors: out of bed on time, washing up, brushing teeth, making the bed, eating breakfast, and leaving the house. What is required varies some from family to family, but it's basically the same job. Believe it or not, these awful morning situations can often be shaped up rather quickly using some of the principles outlined before in this book.

The No-Talking and No-Emotion still apply—even if you haven't had your first cup of coffee.

For the Little Ones

With most kids aged two to four, you'll have to help them get ready and supervise closely. They just can't sustain the activity for that long. Use a lot of Sloppy PVF during the process.

For other children up to about age nine, using charting plus a kitchen timer can be very helpful. Stickers can be used (or numbers if the child prefers). The child's favorite sticker is earned for a super job of getting ready, and their next most favorite sticker for a good job. No sticker means "You blew it, better luck tomorrow."

If you are using the timer, the best performance and best sticker can be for getting ready in a certain reasonable amount of time. Remember that doing well involves not only completing the required activities of washing and dressing, but also doing it as much as possible by oneself and without complaining. A lot of parents also find that not letting the kids watch TV until they're ready is a good idea. Some also don't eat breakfast until they're ready, though you don't want to send them off to school hungry.

Desperate?

Once upon a time there was a mother who was getting more and more fed up with her four year old's fooling around in the morning and never being ready for preschool. The boy was quite bright, but he just never seemed to get going. Whenever the car pool ride came, she was always dressing him at the last minute.

One day Mom finally decided she'd had it with the yelling and screaming and lack of cooperation. It was her day to drive the kids, and—as usual—it was time to go and her son was in his pajamas watching TV. So she did the ultimate: she took him to preschool in his pajamas. The amazed little fellow spent the whole morning of two and one-half hours with his peers—all the time dressed in his pajamas!

A much more relaxed Mom later reported that that was the last time she had any trouble with him getting ready for school.

Such a method is not for the faint-hearted. But neither is what we're about to suggest next for the older children.

Up and Out for Older Kids

For nine year olds and up, the program involves some semi-drastic alterations in the morning routine, and the kids are often shocked into changing.

First of all, it is important to realize that most of these kids either want to go to school and/or they would be embarrassed if they didn't show up or were late. So if they dilly-dally around in the morning, they are going to have some trouble with someone in the car pool, or with the principal or teachers at school. Most kids don't want this, so we use the threat of these natural consequences to shape them up.

Here's how it works. You explain to the kids that from now on it will be their job to get themselves up and out in the morning. *You will neither supervise them or nag.* You can put out clothes for them the night before, if necessary. If you have been waking them up, go out and buy an alarm clock and show them how to use it.

You make it clear to the kids that getting up, getting dressed, washing up, eating breakfast, and leaving on time will be *their* job. If you wish, you can chart them on how well they do, but you cannot say anything to them while they are getting ready, other than casual conversation.

Many parents can't stand this—it drives them crazy to watch the kids fooling around at a late hour, so we have them take their coffee and retire to the bedroom so they don't have to watch.

Breakfast is optional. You can put something out if that's your usual routine, but you *can't remind them to eat it.* Or they can just get their own if they want. Most kids won't die from missing breakfast. When they leave, you say nothing about coats, hats, or gloves, unless there is danger of frostbite.

If the kids fight, you can ignore it or count them if it gets too bad, but that's all. If it's close to time to leave, they may be timed out for only a couple of minutes (or take away TV minutes for later).

What you are doing is teaching the kids some independence and invoking a sacred rule of psychology: Sometimes Learning the Hard Way is the Best Way to Learn. The lessons sink in more when you get burned a few times than they do when you simply hear a lecture. So you have to be willing to *let the kids get burned.*

What does this mean? It means being late to school a few times, being embarrassed, and having to explain to the principal or teacher what happened. It means suddenly realizing at 7:50 that you're not dressed and that Mom didn't remind you that your car pool ride or bus was coming at 8:00. It means getting to school and realizing you forgot your math book at home because you were late leaving. It means blowing your stack at your mother a few times because she's not nagging you anymore to get ready on time, or because she won't write you an excuse note.

This has quite a bit of impact on most kids, and if the parents are consistent, don't talk, and let the kids get burned, the children will shape up in a few days. Then things are much more peaceful at home in the morning, and the kids are much more responsible kids.

By the way, kids have four main ways of getting to school: car pool, bus, walking, or riding bikes. When you are within walking distance of the school, the up and out program is the easiest. With car pools or bus, you may have to drive the kids if they don't make it. For most kids this isn't a problem—they don't get dependent on you driving all the time, especially if they're late. Remember not to lecture them on the way to school if you do have to drive them.

Say nothing.

If you're charting along with the program, use Sloppy PVF for good performances and review the chart at least once a week. You *can* discuss the problem—listen, give brief suggestions, modify things, etc.—at times other than when the kids are getting ready in the morning.

Skeptical?

Many parents, before using this procedure, think their kids will be indifferent to it. They think the kid really doesn't care whether or not he gets to school on time. Part of the reason they think this is because the kid has said it. *Never believe a child who says, "I don't care."* They usually mean the opposite and are testing you.

If you are skeptical, try it out and see what happens. Most kids—not all, but most—will respond well. The most important things are to shut up, stay out of it, and be willing to let the kid get burned more than once. If necessary, let the school know what you're doing; most times, they will cooperate with you, especially if you label the procedure "independence training."

What if it doesn't work? You have some other Start behavior tools, remember? Try charting with artificial reinforcers or using the timer.

If it does work? Enjoy another cup of coffee—and the peace and quiet.

Cleaning Rooms
& Eating

C leaning bedrooms may be the chief cause of parent-child quarrels among all Start behavior problems. Many parents become absolutely enraged when they view the scenes of destruction and chaos in their kids' bedrooms:

> "Barbara, GET UP HERE RIGHT THIS MINUTE!"
> "What?"
> "LOOK AT THIS ROOM! I can't even see the CARPET!
> How am I supposed to do your clothes?"

Kids are not naturally neat. Many—if not most—of them are natural slobs. So they will have to be *trained* to clean their rooms. How can you accomplish that? By this time you shouldn't have to be reminded that you won't get them to do it by nagging or giving them the lecture entitled, "Five Reasons Why It's Nice to Have a Clean Room."

Instead, you have several options. If you're creative, you can probably come up with several more. Here are some good ones.

Option 1: Close the Door and Don't Look

Having a clean room is not a life or death matter, and we know of no research that indicates that kids who didn't keep their rooms neat grow up to be homeless people, criminals or have a higher divorce rate. Besides, whose room is it? You don't have to live in it, so just ask the child to keep the door closed so you don't have to be aggravated. If you have a handicapped child or one who's very difficult anyway, why add one more hassle to your problems? You have bigger things to worry about.

Option 1 is quite legitimate, but there are two problems with it: 1) most parents find it unacceptable, and 2) what about dirty dishes and laundry left in the room?

If you don't want to use Option 1, there will be more suggestions in a minute. As for dirty dishes and clothes, you can use other Start behavior tactics: the timer, charting, or the 1-2-3 (if the dishes or clothes can be picked up in less than two minutes). Some parents whose kids are older simply tell the children that any clothes that don't make it to the laundry or hamper simply don't get washed. That's natural consequences.

The docking system can also be helpful. You go and get the dirty clothes or dishes from their room, but you charge them for your labor. You'll feel better about having to do it, but make sure you keep your mouth shut about the whole operation. Keep the fees reasonable.

Option 2: The Weekly Cleanup Routine

With this method, the kids have to clean their rooms only once a week, but according to your specifications. You might tell them that the following has to be done: pick up, clothes in hamper, make bed, etc. (no windows). A specific day is chosen, such as Saturday morning, and the child doesn't go out or do anything else until his room is done and you've checked him out. You can check him out on a chart if you wish.

Since cleaning the room is a Start behavior, you are rewarding the child right after the cleaning with both freedom and Sloppy PVF. Many parents have tried something like the Weekly Cleanup Routine, but they often ruin it by getting into a hassle with the child at checkout. Remember not to argue about what needs to be done, and try to make the specifications clear to begin with. For example:

"I'm done with my room. Can I go out now?"

"Your bed's not finished."

"Whatta ya mean? That's good enough."

Mom turns to walk away.

"What's the matter with it?"

"That's 1."

"Oh, for Pete's sake!!" Goes to finish bed.

This Mom had already explained before that the bed had to be neatly made, so there was no need for further talk. The kid starts testing using the Badgering tactic, and Mom uses the 1-2-3 on it after ignoring it once. If the youngster winds up back in his room with a 3 count, that's fine because he'll have five minutes to make his bed.

Option 3: Daily Charting

For parents who are more fastidious about cleanliness, the child's room can be charted every day using either the star system (for younger kids) or the 1-5 rating system (for older kids). The child can be informed that the rating will take place every night right before bed.

Keep in mind that you're probably asking for a lot of trouble trying to do this every day, so if you insist on doing this, be nice! Use a lot of Sloppy PVF if the job is done well, and don't expect perfection.

Option 4: The Kitchen Timer

The Close the Door and Don't Look method applies to the kids' rooms. It doesn't apply to the rest of your house! It does not mean the children can keep your kitchen, family room or dining room constantly piled up with all their things. Kitchen counters and dining room tables are such convenient dumping grounds.

The timer is helpful for cleaning rooms (including family rooms), especially when the job has to be done right away. If a surprise guest is coming over, you may not have much time to play around. When using the timer like this, it's perfectly OK to add an artificial reward if the room is done within a certain time, or even an artificial punishment if it's not. Use the Docking System if you feel you are getting stuck with everything.

Eating

Mealtimes can be particularly taxing when a family has one or more children. General fidgetiness plus a little sibling rivalry, plus a few other problems, sometimes make dinnertime a nightmare.

Oddly enough, many families seem to feel that there is a state law or something that dictates that every family eat supper together each and every night of the year. This is the time for "family togetherness" or the time for each person to "share his or her day" with everyone else. Sometimes, however, it becomes the time for everyone to share their hostilities. Tempers as well as appetites can be lost, and the whole affair is anything but pleasant and relaxing.

What can a parent do to improve this situation? One solution, obviously, is to not eat together every night. Though some people consider this sacrilegious, it sure beats fighting all the time. Now you only have to fight every other night! Seriously, sometimes you can feed the kids first and let them eat in front of the TV for once. Or let everyone eat wherever they want to, as long as they bring back their dishes. Then Mom and Dad eat in the kitchen or have a peaceful dinner together later.

Another approach when eating together—especially if the kids horse around too much at the table—is this: first get out a kitchen timer and set it for 20 minutes. Then tell everyone they have to finish in that time. If they do, they get their dessert. If they goof around, they get counted. If they hit a count of three, they are timed out for five minutes while the 20 minute timer keeps on ticking. Don't do a lot of prodding or nagging about eating, such as, "Come on now, don't forget the timer's ticking" or "Quit that goofing around and get down to eating, young man!" (How are you going to finish your own meal if you're talking all the time?)

What if the timer rings and they're not done? No dessert yet. The plate goes into the kitchen and onto the counter. After a half hour has expired, they have the opportunity to finish the meal if they wish. It can be nuked quickly in the microwave if necessary. If they don't ever eat the rest of it, fine, but no dessert. Some parents throw the rest of the dinner down the disposal when the timer hits 20 minutes, but this seems a little harsh.

Stay on your toes when a hungry little thing who didn't finish their dinner puts the hit on you for some dessert later:

> "I'm ready for my dessert now."
> "You'll have to finish your dinner first, honey."
> "It's all cold now."
> "We can just heat it in the microwave for a few seconds and it'll
>   be good as new."
> "I didn't like it anyway. I want just a little dessert."
> "Now you know the rules, dear, you have to finish what's on
>   your plate first. Remember, we didn't give you that much in
>   the first place."
> "I never get anything!"
> "What are you talking about! Now that's enough of that! Either
>   finish your dinner or stop bugging me."
> "I hate you!"

Unfortunate waste of time and very hard on a relationship. It should have gone like this:

> "I'm ready for my dessert now."
> "You'll have to finish your dinner first, honey."
> "It's all cold now."
> "We can just heat it in the microwave for a few seconds and it'll
>   be good as new."
> "I didn't like it anyway. I want just a little dessert."
> "That's 1."
> "Then I'll go to bed starving!" (Walks away)

Much better. Think about dinnertime for a while. It should be a pleasant experience, and with a little planning you can enjoy your evenings a lot more.

15

Homework & Practicing

Homework hassles can make school nights miserable for the whole family. The typical scene involves junior sitting at the kitchen table staring out the window with a sour look on his face. His sister sits in the other room smugly watching TV. Mom and Dad check in to the kitchen every five or ten minutes to badger the reluctant scholar.

For some families these battles can go on for two, three, or four hours per night. People begin to dread the evening, relationships are strained severely, and the child in question learns to hate schoolwork more and more. There are no easy answers to the homework problem, and children's needs vary depending upon their intelligence and the presence of handicaps such as learning disabilities and Attention Deficit Disorder. There are some ways, though, of making things more tolerable and more productive.

What Not to Do

Don't go around asking the child every five minutes if they have homework or if they've started it yet. Instead try to pick the best time to start and stick with it as much as possible.

Don't interrupt the youngster in the middle of their favorite TV show and tell them it's time to begin. There's *no* better way to get *no* cooperation.

Don't let the would-be student do work with the TV on. Believe it or not, a radio or stereo may be OK because it provides consistent background noise, but the television is always out to get your attention with something new.

Don't let the homework time change each day if you can avoid it. One of the best ways of setting things up is to have the child come home, get a snack and goof off for about one-half hour to forty-five minutes, and then sit down and try to finish before dinner.

What to do? Consider trying the following steps in order (you can combine them as you go), and be sure to use plenty of tailored Sloppy PVF along with whatever you are doing.

Natural Consequences

If you are having trouble with homework for the first time—say with a fourth grader—consider using Natural Consequences first. That means do nothing. Keep your mouth shut and see if the child and the teacher can work things out. If this doesn't seem to be working after a few weeks, then go on to the next step.

Natural Consequences is obviously not the method to use if you have been having homework problems for years and years.

An Assignment Sheet

Assignment sheets or notebooks can be extremely helpful. They tell you exactly what work is due for each subject. Some schools have even instituted "Homework Hotlines," where forgetful but fortunate kids can call in after hours to find out what their assignments are.

The idea of the assignment sheet, of course, is that after the child does the work parents can check it out against the list of items to be done. If this is the procedure you are thinking of using, you must routinely include in it two basic principles: the "PNP Method" and the "Rough Checkout." Failure to do so will result in unnecessary evening misery.

The PNP Method

Suppose your son or daughter has just completed their midweek spelling pretest. There are ten words on the list and they spelled nine correctly and misspelled one. When they bring you their paper, your job, naturally, is to first point out to them the word they spelled wrong. Right?

Wrong! PNP stands for "Positive-Negative-Positive." This means that whenever any kid brings any piece of schoolwork to you, the first thing out of your mouth must be something good. This means some version of Sloppy PVF. Then, after saying something nice about their effort, you may throw in something negative *if it's absolutely necessary*. Finally, you conclude your insightful remarks with something positive again.

Using the spelling pretest as an example, you would first say something like, "Gee, you spelled 'consideration' correctly. That's a pretty hard word. And you also got 'appearance' right. In fact, there's only one word on here that I can see you didn't get. Not bad."

You might stop here and try to kill them with suspense. See if they're dying to find out what the wrong word is. If they're not, you can tell them. Then end the conversation with another positive comment.

Remember the rule: every time they bring you some work to check, the first thing you say must be positive, even if it's only the fact that they brought the work to you. Kids will never want to bring you anything if your first response is consistently to shoot from the hip with criticism.

The Rough Checkout

The Rough Checkout idea is based on the fact that 8 PM is no time for scholastic perfection. You have worked all day, and your child has also put in just about the equivalent of a day on a full-time job —before they started their homework!

Unless there is some major indication to the contrary, therefore, if their work is anywhere near 80% neat, correct, and thorough, consider calling it a day and let your youngster and teacher worry about it tomorrow. This is doubly true for ADD or LD children who already have a bad enough time as it is with school. If, on the other hand, the child is generally a very good student (not potentially, but actually), you might consider raising the required percentage to 90 or so.

A mother once came in to a psychologist reporting that her 12 year old son seemed to be getting depressed, more irritable, and more distant from everyone in the family. It turned out that homework was a major problem every night. This was the procedure: the boy would finish his homework and then bring it to his father for checkout. That was the good news. The bad news was that if it was not absolutely perfect the father would tear it all up!

When asked how many times—on the average—the dad was tearing up the kid's homework, the mother said about three times per evening. No wonder the boy was getting demoralized.

The psychologist insisted on seeing the father. Dad blustered into the office insisting that his son was going to learn to do things right and that he was going to master his subjects, etc., etc. The psychologist replied that the boy was indeed learning a lot: he was learning to hate his father, to hate schoolwork, and to hate himself, and, if this nightly routine was continued, it could easily produce a high school dropout in four years. That was the end of that.

If the youngster's work is about 80% neat, correct, and complete, use the PNP procedure. You don't have to tell them that it's perfect, just that it's good enough. Some perfectionists may squirm at this, but they should try to stay in touch with the emotional realities of childhood.

Charting

Charting lends itself very well to homework. Here's an easy system that can be used.

Since it's usually the older kids who are having trouble with homework, a five point scale can be used instead of stickers. Five is high and one is low. The child can earn one point each for the following things:

Neat - 1 point
Correct - 1 point
Thorough - 1 point
No complaining - 1 point

Starting on your own - 1 point

The kids can get each of the first three points by doing better than whatever approximate percentage of neatness, correctness, and completeness you have required. The last point is the crucial one: if you can get a child to start on their own, the battle is half won. You can set up friendly incentive games with this last point. For example, three days in a row of starting on your own at the proper time earns a bonus point. Or, starting more than fifteen minutes early and finishing in a reasonable amount of time earns a bonus point. Or, put on your thinking cap and see what other schemes you can come up with.

Remember that for many kids with academic handicaps, you may very well have to use artificial reinforcers to help motivate the child over the homework hurdle.

Also, don't forget that kitchen timer. Sometimes it can be used to help break up the work into smaller, manageable pieces. If the child complains that the ticking bothers them (most don't), use some kind of sand hourglass.

Practicing Obnoxious Musical Instruments

The tactics for getting kids to practice follow the same logic as those for homework. Avoid the same "don'ts" and try natural consequences first if the child is just starting out. The PNP method still applies—make sure any of your comments are started with positive reinforcement, then add the negative if it's absolutely necessary.

The spirit of the Rough Checkout also applies in the sense that 8:30 PM is no time for perfection. Charting also can help a lot. For some kids just putting on the chart the number of minutes they practiced can be enough to keep them going. For others artificial reinforcers may be necessary, but remember that the points for no complaining and—especially—for starting on your own are very helpful.

Now that the homework and practicing are out of the way, it's time for bed!

16

Bedtime & Nighttime Waking

For many parents, putting the kids to bed is a daily nightmare. In theory, bedtime may be nine o'clock, but at ten thirty the children are still wandering around the house, asking for drinks, or going to the bathroom for the twentieth time. This may be accompanied by a good deal of arguing and screaming, which only serves the purpose of making sure that everyone stays awake to watch the late movie together.

With a little thought, this kind of end to the evening can be avoided. Many of the Start behavior tactics can be used for bedtime, and if you put them together you can produce the Basic Bedtime Method (2-3 year olds will need a little extra help).

Basic Bedtime Method

The first thing that needs to be done is to set a bedtime for the kids and to stick to it as much as possible. The time may vary, of course, depending on whether or not it's a school night or a weekend, or whether it's during the school year or summertime. Let's assume that you have a nine year old, and you decide that nine o'clock will be the time to go to bed.

At eight thirty you set a timer for 30 minutes and tell the child that it's time to get ready for bed. This means that the youngster must do everything required to prepare for bed—on his own—and then report to you. (If the child is two or three, you'll have to help them get ready, but the same rewards/consequences apply). If the child has in fact completed all the necessary tasks, you dish out a little Sloppy PVF. Then the rest of the time that is left between eight thirty and nine is time for a story or time to simply sit and talk with the child.

This serves three purposes. It is an immediate reinforcer for the child's doing a good job of getting ready for bed. It is also a good opportunity for you to spend a little quiet time together; most kids still value this quite a bit. And finally, this time helps the kids quiet down and get more in the mood for going to sleep. You certainly wouldn't want them running around and yelling right before they're supposed to hit the sack.

If you have trouble coming up with the list of all that needs to be done, just think of all the things they usually tell you *they haven't done* after they are in bed, and you'll have it right away.

"I'm hungry."

"I'm scared."

"I need a drink."

"I have to go to the bathroom."

"These pajamas itch."

"There's a burglar in the basement."

"When's daddy coming home?"

Etc., etc., etc. All this should be taken care of and discussed if necessary.

One caution here. Don't lie down on the bed. This has nothing to do with anything Freudian or sexual. It just so happens that there is a biological law that says: if you are over twenty-five years of age and it's past eight o'clock in the evening, and you spend more than three minutes in a horizontal position, you're gone! The kids will love having you sleeping next to them, but they may get dependent on it and it goofs up their bedtime routine.

When nine o'clock rolls around, tuck the child in, kiss them goodnight, and leave the room. At this point some parents say, "How naive you are. The kid is right behind me!"

Getting Out of Bed

Some kids just can't seem to stay in bed after you tuck them in. You put them down and they get up. You try to go about your business. They are always coming up with some new reason for getting out of bed.

What you should do about this is based on a basic principle: *if a child gets out of bed, the longer they are out of bed and/or the longer they stay up, the more reinforcement they get for doing this.* The only conclusion, therefore, is that you have to cut them off at the pass. It is no fun, but this is no time for wishful thinking—or ridiculous conversations about why they should stay in bed. What you do is park yourself in a chair in the doorway to their bedroom. Get a good book if you want. Sit with your back to them and don't talk no matter what they say. If they get out of bed and come to you, take them gently by the arm or pick them up and put them back.

If you have a child who is a bit older (seven or older), you might be able to use charting to help the youngster stay in bed. Be careful with this, however, because there is unique problem when it comes to bedtime. In general, rewards and punishments are most effective when they are given out immediately. Some studies have shown that even a few minutes delay in administering consequences can sometimes have a dramatic effect on their usefulness.

If you are using charting with bedtime, you cannot tell the child right away how he did. In fact, if he does really well, he shouldn't be awake for you to be able to talk to him about the whole thing. Therefore, there must be quite a long delay before he finds out how you rated him (like the next morning), and you may find that this reduces the effectiveness of the procedure.

Nighttime Waking

Many children go through periods from time to time when they wake up at night. Some kids may get out of bed a dozen or more times, while others will just make noise or say something and then go back to sleep. Nighttime problems are among the hardest to handle, because in the middle of the night most parents aren't quite in their right minds—and neither are their kids! It's also very aggravating to be awakened from a sound sleep, and it can have a very bad effect on your next day at work.

Handling these situations incorrectly can make things worse very rapidly, and the number of times the kid wakes up can get more frequent and more traumatic for everybody. If people don't get enough sleep, their mood on the next day is affected, and then they get even more upset during the night.

There are several guidelines that have proven to be very effective in calming these nighttime episodes down and getting the child back to sleeping through.

1: Accept some periodic waking as normal

Treat it as a temporary stage. This will help you be less upset. Obviously, if it's been going on for the last four years, it's not a temporary "stage."

2: No-Talking and No-Emotion

These rules apply doubly for nighttime, because talking and emotion—especially anger—wake everyone up. Ever tried to sleep when you're furious? It doesn't work. Even asking the child what's wrong is most often useless, because he's groggy, not in his right mind, and can't tell you much. This applies to fears and bad dreams, too; try to discuss them the next day if you can.

3: Assume the child may have to go to the bathroom

Even though they don't or can't say it, many kids are awakened by the urge to go. But they're so sleepy they aren't sure what the feeling is and can't verbalize. So try putting them on the toilet and see what happens. Don't ask them unless you know from vast experience they are capable of giving you an accurate answer.

4: Be gentle and quiet

Handle and guide them softly as you stagger through the dark. Why should it be dark?

5: No lights!

Lights wake you and the child up more. Your eyes should be dark adapted in the middle of the night, so try to stagger around without turning on anything.

6: Don't go to the child's room unless you have to

When do you have to? If they are really screaming or unless they come to you first. Some kids will make a little noise and then go back to sleep—give them a chance to do this.

7: Don't let the child sleep with you on a regular basis

It can become a habit that's hard to break later. It's true, it may be the easiest way to quiet them down right at the moment—and staying in bed certainly is tempting—but you will pay for it later. One exception: if there's a terrible storm going on outside, let them sleep on the floor next to your bed with sleeping bags and pillows. They'll do it. Otherwise, get them back in their room.

Now let's put these rules together and go through some possible sequences that might occur.

Mark, age 9

Mark has been sleeping regularly through the night. Tuesday night, however, after watching a rather scary movie on TV, he says a few short, disconnected sentences at 2:45 AM and is restless in bed. You wait for a few minutes to see if he'll wake up or get up, but you don't go in his room. After a few minutes he goes back to sleep and is peaceful for the rest of the night.

Jennie, age 6

Jennie has been restless in bed for a few nights, but hasn't gotten up. Thursday night, however, she appears at your bedside, shakes you by the arm a bit, and says she's scared. You say nothing, but get up, put your arm around her shoulders, and steer her to the bathroom. She sits on the toilet for awhile, but no lights are turned on. Then you steer her gently back to bed, tuck her in, and give her a kiss. You wait for a second, see that she's falling asleep, then go back to bed.

Jim, age 4

Jim has been getting up several times a night. He won't go back to bed by himself and starts raising a ruckus if you tell him to go back to bed. You can't tell if he's frightened or what. If you take him to his room, he cries or starts yelling if you try to leave. He says he wants to sleep with you. You know he's not sick, because he was just checked out by your pediatrician.

This is a more difficult situation, obviously, than the first two examples. You don't want him to wake up everyone in the house, but you don't like the idea of giving in to his testing either. What should you do?

When Jim appears at your bedside, you escort him to the bathroom first—no lights, no talking, etc. Then you take him to his room, put him in bed, tuck him in. Now you know he'll cry if you try to leave, so before he gets a chance to do that you get a chair, park yourself in it by the bed, and wait till he goes back to sleep. This is not fun at all, but it works best. If you've done the other things right—like no lights or arguing—he should still be somewhat sleepy.

With some kids this procedure must be repeated several times a night for several weeks before they start sleeping through again. Our record so far for most times getting up in one night is 17! If you think you'll have to sit by the bed, get the chair ready beforehand. After a few nights, you can gradually start moving the chair out of the room, so you wind up sitting just outside the door where the child can't see you. If he asks if you're still there, make some noise like sniffing or moving around, but try not to talk. Soon after that, you shouldn't have to even sit in the chair.

Suzie, age 8

Suzie sleeps almost all the way through, but likes to get up at 5:30 AM and come to see you. She looks like she's ready for the day. You've told her to go back to bed, but she won't do it.

There are several things you can try. First, consider adjusting her bedtime back an hour, say from 8 to 9: she may not need that much sleep. Use the Basic Bedtime Method. Second, make sure her room isn't getting too much sunlight too early—that always helps kids wake up.

Third, you can try the procedure from the third example. Put her on the toilet and then see if she'll go back to sleep. If it's obvious that she won't, you will next try to train her to play in her room instead of waking you or someone else up.

How do you do this? Try a combination of charting and the 1-2-3. Make a chart—using stars or numbers—that will keep a record of how well she does in the morning *playing by herself* and *not waking anyone up*. She is to stay in her room if she's younger, but may go downstairs and watch TV if she's older or it's not ridiculously early in the morning. Give her her score on the chart and some Sloppy PVF when you get up.

If she forgets and comes to you at 5:30, you say calmly, "Go back to bed, that's 1." Going back to bed at this point is a START behavior that takes less than two minutes. If she argues or doesn't go, you may count her out, and you may have to escort her back to her room. No extra talking and no emotion.

Physical pain can certainly wake kids up at night, so if they haven't had a physical lately and they start waking up at night, it might be a good idea to have them checked out. In the meantime you use the procedures described here. Share the joy, if possible: if Mom and Dad are both available, take turns getting up. Sometimes it's fairly grueling, but it pays off in the end.

Questions

What if the youngster is not ready for bed and it's nine o'clock?

You can put them in bed with their clothes on. Take off their shoes so they're more comfortable. For the little ones (2 or 3) you might want to just put their pajamas on them. And remember to not get caught up in the very tempting alternative of lecturing them about what they should have done. It's late, you're tired and they're tired, and it's all too easy to slip up.

Someone told me that floor fans help kids sleep. What kind of sense does that make?

Believe it or not, floor fans do help some children go to sleep and stay asleep. Floor fans produce what is sometimes called "white noise," which is simply a monotonous, repetitive sound that is not disturbing. White noise, however, does tend to cover other night noises that may keep kids awake, such as a door closing, a car going by, a toilet flushing, a TV going, etc. Some people also feel that the noise of a fan is in itself a kind of natural tranquilizer that encourages sleep.

Remember, though, it's the noise your looking for—not the wind— so don't blow the fan right on anybody. Actually, in the summer the air circulation can help too. White noise also makes it easier for you to sneak out of their room at 3 AM, after you've gotten up with them for the second time!

Part V:

More Serious Stop Behavior

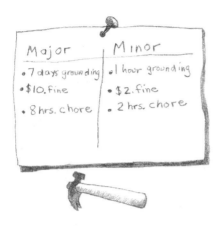

17

The Major/Minor System

S uppose your neighbor comes over on a summer day and tells you that your nine year old son just put a rock through his garage window. Deliberately. That's obviously Stop behavior, but it wouldn't make much sense to run to the back door and say, "Greg, that's 1." "That's 3, take 5" also would seem a little mild. Some punishment is called for, but you still want to avoid a lot of excess talking and emotion because you know that can make things worse.

More Serious Stop Behavior

There are a lot of things that can come up from time to time that are too serious for the 1-2-3, but that still require some action on your part to train the kids not to repeat them. Included in this list are things like lying, stealing, serious fights, major behavioral problems at school, breaking things, losing things, not coming home, and so on. Fortunately, there is a very simple punishment system that you can set up which can handle these problems well and with a minimum of upset. It's called the Major/ Minor System.

The Major/Minor System starts by simply classifying any type of Stop behavior as either Major or Minor, depending upon how serious you think it is. (The "Very Minor" things you're already handling with the 1-2-3). Actually, it's often helpful to have a Major/Medium/Minor system so things aren't so black and white.

Once you have come up with your classifications, you decide upon a punishment for each category, and each time the offense occurs you just dish out that punishment. It saves a lot of effort and deliberation, and it also can let the kids know beforehand what the consequences are for certain behavior. Punishments usually involve things like groundings, fines, restrictions of privileges such as TV time, and extra work around the house.

The punishments for Major offenses are greater than the punishments for Medium ones, and Medium consequences are bigger than those for Minor problems. Keep in mind that Minor offenses are still more serious than countable things such as arguing, yelling, teasing, whining, and so on. One family, for example, set up the following system for their nine year old son:

Major Offenses

Stealing, fighting, breaking something valuable, coming home more than three hours late, playing with fire

Medium Offenses

Coming home 1-3 hours late, lying

Minor Offenses

Coming home less than 1 hour late, losing or breaking something valued at less than $10

Note that not all possible misbehaviors are listed. These were the things these parents were having trouble with with this boy. They set up the following consequences, and agreed that for all but Major offenses the boy could pick the consequence.

Major Consequences

7 days grounding in room with no TV—after school and weekends, $10 fine or pay back double the value of stolen article, no TV for 2 weeks, 8 hours work around the house

Medium Consequences

3 days grounding in room with no TV, $5 fine, 4 hours of chores

Minor Consequences

1 hour grounding in room, $2 fine, 2 hours work around the house

You don't need to set up the system unless you already have some specific problems. When the problem occurs, then, it is simply categorized and the consequence determined. No yelling or screaming by Mom and Dad, though sometimes a *short* explanation may be in order. For each misbehavior, one (not all) of the possible punishments listed is administered. Sometimes we even let the kid pick which one he wants.

You can adjust the Major/Minor System to some extent after you set it up, but be careful and try not to make punishments so harsh that they backfire. One family, for example, had a system like the one described above. Then one day they found out that their kid had stolen a bike! The Major punishments didn't seem big enough for this, so they told the boy he was grounded for a year. This will not work, and they probably won't enforce it well after a while, anyway. It's better to have something like grounding for a month and pay back the value of the bike.

What if the kid does something that you didn't put on the original Major/Minor lists? You just classify it as Major or Minor and then give the corresponding punishment. If you've been having a real problem with repeated offenses, you can also make a chart that keeps track of the number of days in a row that are free of trouble. If the problems continue, it might be time for evaluation and counseling with a professional.

Caution

Several things should be kept in mind about the Major/Minor plan: First, it can't be used effectively with two to three year olds. They won't get the idea.

Second, it's a good idea to write down the plan—and perhaps even sign it—so everyone remembers exactly what it is.

Third, you usually don't need to do the Major/Minor unless you've already been having a fair amount of trouble with a child. If your youngster basically is a good kid and rarely gets into trouble, then one day is two hours late for dinner or gets into a fight, you may want to find out what happened first. Then, if you think it was bad judgment on their part, a stern warning not to repeat the action may be enough.

Fourth, bigger problems like this make you madder. Keep explanations short and sweet, and be sure to active listen (Chapter 20) when you need more information from your child. Blowing your stack can ruin the effectiveness of whatever consequences you—or your child—select.

18

Lying

It's the truth. Some kids will lie from time to time. This can drive some parents crazy. The school calls at one o'clock to tell you that your ten year old son, Tom, got into a fight with a boy named Davey Smith at lunch. At 3:45 PM Tom comes home. The conversation then goes like this:

> "How was your day?" you ask.
> "Good, great sandwich you made me for lunch."
> "Speaking of lunchtime, how did it go?" you inquire.
> "Fine, we played baseball."
> "Anything unusual happen?
> "Not that I can think of."
> "OK, listen, young man. You're lying to me. I got a call from the school today...etc., etc."

The parent is "cornering" the youngster. Got to find out what really happened and also see if he'll tell the truth. Is this the right way to handle this situation?

Two Kinds of Lying

First of all, there are basically two kinds of lies. The first is making up stories that are designed to impress other people and build one's ego. The second—and by far the most common—is lying to get out of or avoid trouble. Kids will often lie about homework, for example, so they don't have to do it; or they may lie about it because they forgot to bring their books home. They may also deny having gotten into a fight or having stolen or broken something.

Second, when it comes to dealing with lying, the first thing parents should remember is not to treat lying as if it were the equivalent of homicide or adultery! It certainly isn't a good thing to do, but it's not the end of the world. Far too many parents get so upset about it that they communicate to the child that he is really a horrible person for having done it.

What Should You Do?

The first rule is don't badger or corner children! Imagine you give a child the third degree, for example, about whether or not he has homework. He denies it six times and then finally, after your seventh question, he admits that he has some. What has happened? You are furious by this time, but you also have just given the child six times to practice lying! You may think to yourself, "Sooner or later he'll realize he can't fool me and he'll give it up." Wrong. Many children will continue to take the easy, short-term way out if possible, and will simply attempt to become better liars.

Look at it like this. You either know the truth or you don't. So, first of all, if you don't know what is going on, ask once and don't badger. It's a good idea here to not ask "impulsively," meaning on the spur of the moment. Many kids simply respond by responding impulsively back to you, but their real desire is just to end the conversation, get rid of you, and stay out of trouble.

If you are going to ask, you might say something like, "I want you to tell me the story of what happened, but not right now. Think about it a while and we'll talk in fifteen minutes." If they tell you the story and you find out later that the child lied, punish them for whatever the offense was as well as for the lie (see the Major/Minor System in Chapter 17). No lectures or tantrums. Deal with the problem and try to fix things—as much as you can—so that lying does not feel as necessary to the child. If he continually lies about homework, for example, work out some kind of communication with the teacher, such as a daily assignment sheet. Then use the tactics described in Chapter 15.

Second, if you do know what has happened, tell him what you know and deal with it. If he has done something wrong that you know about, simply punish him reasonably for that and end the conversation with "I'm sure you'll do better next time." Some parents still prefer to ask the child what happened—even when they already know—and this is OK if you do it right. You should say something like, "I got a call from the school today about an incident at lunch. I'm going to ask you to tell me the story, but not right now. I want you to think about it for a while, then when you're ready you can tell me, but remember I already pretty much know what happened."

Lying is not good, but it certainly isn't the end of the world either. It happens from time to time. It doesn't mean that your kids don't love you or that they are bound to grow up to become professional criminals. Frequent emotional overreactions on your part, however, when combined with badgering and cornering, can produce over the years an Accomplished Liar.

Part VI

Part VI:

Your Child's Self-Esteem

19

10 Steps for Building Self-Esteem

Every parent wants to help their children to have good self-esteem. Throughout life a realistic and positive self-esteem is essential to maintaining a good mood, asserting oneself with confidence, getting along with others, and even keeping physically healthy. How can a parent make sure that their children will think well of themselves?

This is obviously easier said than done—and you don't have total control over the matter—but here are ten essential steps that can help you go a long way.

1. Get Real!

"Get real" means two things here. The first is that a child's self-esteem will never be based on some kind of gimmick. It will be based on their entire life. A little bit of this or that "self-esteem technique" won't even scratch the surface if the youngster's whole life is a disaster. Sometimes, reading articles or books about self-esteem, you kind of get the feeling there's some way of tricking a child into thinking well of themselves in spite of the fact that they're flunking in school, have no friends, and are a major pain to manage at home. It isn't true.

Second—and perhaps unfortunately—you don't have total control over how your kids turn out or over their ultimate level of self-esteem. You can do the best you can, but it's important to realize that many other factors contribute to their development. Innate physical and mental capabilities, for example, are strongly influenced by heredity (you don't control the genes you give your kids). Children are also influenced by others outside the family, by their schools and teachers, and by the times in which they live. Just plain good and bad luck can play a large role.

Kids, therefore, are not like putty in your hands.

Why is it important to realize this? Because—like it or not—your self-esteem as a parent has a lot to do with how your kids are doing. If you are expecting the impossible of yourself, of course, you will suffer. You also run the risk of putting pressure on your children to accomplish or to be what may not be possible for them.

2. Manage the Two "Curses"

It sometimes seems that whoever designed us as parents did the job backwards, because what we tend to naturally think and what we tend to naturally do very often come out unrealistic or negative or both. These two problems are sort of like biological or ingrained curses. The first curse makes our thinking overly perfectionistic, and the second curse can be summed up in the phrase, "Angry parents make noise, happy ones keep quiet."

If you do ten things in the course of a day, and you handle nine correctly while you mess up one, which do you think about at the end of the day. Most people stew about the thing they messed up. They take for granted what they did right and forget about it.

But forget about a mistake? No way. For some reason we just seem to be much more impressed by what goes wrong than by what goes right. Isn't this what the news on TV is all about?

Unfortunately, evaluating one's own behavior with this "newscaster" mentality has a predictable effect on self-esteem, and it certainly isn't good. This natural tendency toward magnified self-criticism makes people discouraged and even depressed.

What does this have to do with my kids, you ask? The interesting thing here is that if you think this way about yourself, you will tend to treat other family members in the same way. You will be more impressed by the mistakes and failings of your spouse and your children than you will by their good points.

This then helps lead to the second curse, which affects the way we act. Certainly if your mind is more preoccupied with the negative aspects of your children's behavior, you will probably reflect that in what you talk about. But the idea that "angry parents make noise" while "happy parents keep quiet" is based on more than just thinking.

The fact of the matter is that—for biological reasons—anger motivates action (including talking), while contentment does not. Anger produces the "fight or flight" response, which revs up the body to do something. So when the kids irritate you, you are likely to come up with some "fighting words." When the children are playing happily with no problem, however, you are likely not to say anything.

What is one to do about the two curses? First of all, remember that your kids do much more good than bad—they are basically good little people. Second, let your speech and actions reflect that fact by paying attention to the nine other self-esteem steps mentioned here.

3. Good Discipline Is Basic

Unless you know what you're doing when it comes to disciplining the kids and maintaining order in the home, none of the other steps mentioned here will do much good. In fact, you won't even feel like doing any of the rest of them. Good discipline is what *1-2-3 Magic* is all about.

If you don't have your discipline act together, the kids will constantly have you feeling overwhelmed with anger and resentment. You will be yelling and screaming—or perhaps even worse. But kids are just kids. They are erratic and still learning what's what. They are supposed to frustrate you on a regular basis. If you can't take this more or less in stride and handle it, you will communicate to them that they are only a pain in the neck to you. It doesn't take a rocket scientist to figure out what this message will do to their self-esteem.

In addition, research has shown that erratic discipline tends to produce hostile and erratic behavior in children. This then furthers a downward spiral of self-esteem.

Here's a quick check on your home discipline. First ask yourself what the three biggest problems you have with your youngsters are. Perhaps they are sibling rivalry, whining, and bedtime. Next ask yourself what your method is for dealing with each of these problems. If you can't answer fairly quickly, or if your answer is you're not sure, or if what you really do is some version of arguing, yelling, nagging or hitting, then you're in trouble.

And you also, apparently, didn't read this book! Better review it and get started. By the way, if those are your problems, look up sibling rivalry in Chapter 8, whining in Chapter 10, and bedtime in Chapter 16.

4. Treat Any Problems

The development of many children is impaired by emotional, behavioral, or physical problems that can make life much more of a challenge for them. Things such as anxiety disorders, learning disabilities, Attention Deficit Disorder, asthma, or physical handicaps can make kids feel different, hinder their ability to perform normally, and lower self-esteem.

It doesn't seem as though you would even have to mention it, but it is obvious that helping the child deal with these problems as well as possible is critical to the psychological welfare of affected youngsters.

Many parents hold back on doing something, however, for any number of reasons. For one thing, they are not sure if there is a problem or not. For another thing, the child isn't requesting help and may even fight the idea of seeing a doctor. Parents also feel—perhaps correctly—that the very act of "seeking help for a problem" has a negative effect on self-esteem.

Such thinking isn't realistic and is only looking at the short-term. Kids rarely ask to see anyone for these kinds of problems, but they only get one chance to grow up. A good rule of thumb is this: if you have been worrying for more than one year about the possibility that your child suffers from a particular kind of problem and you haven't checked it out, it's past the time to do something. If you check it out and there is a problem, you can do something about it. If you find out there is no problem, you can stop worrying.

5. Positive Reinforcement

It can't be emphasized often enough that kids need positive, supportive comments from you on a frequent and regular basis. See the first Start behavior tactic in Chapter 12.

How about the "quota system"? Each day, every other person in the family (including spouse!) will receive from you three positive comments, such as:

"Good job!"
"Thanks for getting that for me."
"That was really hard for you, but you did it."
"I think you handled that very well."

It doesn't take very long to say these things, but they will be remembered and can make a big difference to someone's self-esteem.

6. Shared Fun

A famous psychologist once said, "Show me two people who have fun together on a regular basis and I'll show you a good relationship." Being together in the same place at the same time and enjoying the same thing is almost the essence of what some people like to refer to as "bonding."

The fun doesn't have to be fancy or expensive. It certainly could be a vacation, but it could also be watching a movie at home, just talking, shopping, playing baseball or going out for a hamburger. Knowing you're going to do something fun with a child helps you get along better beforehand. After it's over, the pleasant memories help you get along better afterward. This is especially true for the older kids (8-12); the little ones (2-3) honestly won't remember too much.

As the parent, try to find something you enjoy too, not just something you tolerate for the sake of your child. And while you're out having a good time, no talking about problems unless the child wants to. Can you manage doing something once a week for at least one hour?

Fun with the entire family is good and necessary. What many parents don't like to hear, however, is that the kind of fun that means the most to the kids is one-on-one. One parent with one child. The bad news here is that it takes more time if you have more than one child. The good news is that the lack of sibling rivalry also makes it more pleasant for Mom or Dad.

7. Plain Old Affection

Verbal and nonverbal expressions of affection also help a child feel good about themselves. Affection put in words is very similar to positive reinforcement, so make sure it is tailored to the child. Some kids like the more obvious kinds and some kids prefer the more subdued and subtle. The little ones may like to sit on your lap for a while. The older ones may prefer a hug or a pat on the back.

8. Expertise Building

Any child feels good about having something that they are good at doing. Helping a youngster find something that they can excel in and nurturing their interest over time can work wonders for self-esteem. Perhaps the child is good at one sport (or several). Maybe they like computers or music. How about reading or writing or school itself?

It's always nice if the child's area of expertise is something that no other child in the family is into, but this, of course, isn't always possible. Nurturing a child's interests and skills also does not mean shoving something down their throat. Nurturing does mean phone calls, chauffeuring, dollars, and watching them do their thing!

9. Non-Evaluation

Parents were put on earth for a lot of reasons: to guide their kids, nurture them, give them a sense of values, and keep them out of trouble. This does not mean that they always have to be on their case!

The 1-2-3 works very well in managing Stop behavior, but the power of the 1-2-3 can be abused. A parent could use it to pick and pick a child to death. Try to decide beforehand what kinds of things you will count. Try also to notice how much your counting changes depending on your mood. Some change may be inevitable, but too much variability will confuse the kids.

It's nice to have quiet times when no one is being evaluated.

10. Active Listening

The last point about fostering self-esteem in children is important enough to merit its own chapter. Active listening may sound rather fancy or even "shrink-like," but it's a great way to get along and one of the most potent ways to help your kids feel confident about themselves.

20

Active Listening

Your ten year old son, Tom, comes running in the door after school and yells, "My music teacher's an idiot!" What should you do?

You could count—after all the kid is screaming. But think about it for a second. He is *not* screaming at you and he *is* upset about something, and you don't know what it is. The priorities here should be to give the child some support and also find out what happened. His being angry is no crime, and this couldn't be testing and manipulation, because you didn't do anything to frustrate him.

This is a time for "active listening." The conversation might go something like this:

Tom: "My music teacher's an idiot!"

Mom: "Tell me what happened."

Tom: "She made me sing in front of the whole stupid class, and only one other kid—a girl—had to do it. She didn't care, but all my friends were laughing at me!"

Mom: "What did she make you sing?"

Tom: "I don't know, some stupid religious hymn or some other completely dumb thing."

Mom: "That must have been awfully embarrassing."

Tom: "I'm going to bomb her car!"

Mom: "Boy, I haven't seen you this mad for a while! So what happened when you had to sing?"

Tom: "She makes me stand in the front of the room, then she plays her idiot piano, and I don't even know the dumb song! I could see Dave was giggling and trying not to laugh. I'd like to see him do it!"

Mom: "So you thought it wasn't very fair for her to make you do it when no one else had to."

Tom: "Yeah. Why are they picking on me all the time? What a dumb school." Tom leaves to get a snack.

Active Listening and Self-esteem

Active listening is a way of listening and talking to someone with sympathy or empathy (the distinction between the two isn't important here). It is very respectful of another's thoughts and feelings, because the listener doesn't just sit there, but instead attempts to see the world through the other person's eyes.

When you are doing this with your child, you are—like the mother above—forgetting your own opinions for a while, suspending judgment, and committing yourself to completely understanding how they saw a particular situation (you don't have to agree with them). In the example here Mom is not thinking to herself that her son is being disrespectful, or that maybe he caused the trouble, or what she will say back to him.

Active listening, therefore, tries to accomplish two things: 1) to understand what another person is saying and thinking—from his or her point of view, and 2) to communicate back and check that understanding with the person doing the talking. The listener is an active participant in the conversation, not someone who just sits and nods from time to time.

Active listening is not easy, but it can be mastered. Once you get past the point of feeling artificial, "parrot like," or too passive, you can sometimes pleasantly knock the kids right off their feet with it. And it is an excellent way of beginning any lengthy, serious conversation when a problem does need to be discussed.

How Do You Do Active Listening?

First, you must get yourself in the proper frame of mind: "I'm going to hear this kid out—even if it kills me— and find out exactly what they think and feel about what's going on." Next there are several different things that can be done, and once you get used to them the whole thing can feel quite natural. These include openers, nonjudgmental questions, reflecting feelings, and perception checks or summaries.

In the example above, here's where these "tactics" appeared:

Tom: "My music teacher's an idiot!"

Mom: "Tell me what happened." **(Opener)**

Tom: "She made me sing in front of the whole stupid class, and only one other kid—a girl—had to do it. She didn't care, but all my friends were laughing at me!"

Mom: "What did she make you sing?" **(Question)**

Tom: "I don't know, some stupid religious hymn or some other completely dumb thing."

Mom: "That must have been awfully embarrassing."
  (Reflecting feeling)

Tom: "I'm going to bomb her car!"

Mom: "Boy, I haven't seen you this mad for a while!
  (Reflecting feeling)

"So what happened when you had to sing?" **(Question)**

Tom: "She makes me stand in the front of the room, then she plays her idiot piano, and I don't even know the dumb song! I could see Dave was giggling and trying not to laugh. I'd like to see him do it!"

Mom: "So you thought it wasn't very fair for her to make you
do it when no one else had to." (**Check/Summary**)

Tom: "Yeah. Why are they picking on me all the time? What a
dumb school." Tom leaves to get something to eat.

Openers

You can start with what are called "openers"—brief comments or questions designed to elicit further information from your child. These comments often require self-control, and are especially difficult when you are caught off guard. They may also appear incredibly passive or wimpy to you, but remember that active listening must precede any problem solving discussion. If discipline or other action is necessary, worry about it after you've gotten the facts.

Openers can be very simple:

"Oh?"
"Wow!"
"Yeah."
"What?"

Anything that communicates that you are ready and willing to listen sympathetically, including nonverbal behavior, such as sitting down next to the youngster or putting down the paper to look at them.

Nonjudgmental Questions

An opener can be a question or it can be some other kind of statement, but usually further questions will be necessary. To be effective, questions must not be loaded or judgmental.

Here are some bad questions:

"Why did you do a stupid thing like that?"
"What were you thinking!?!"
"What's your problem today?"

"Why are you bugging me now about this?"

These questions will inspire argument or silence. Here are some better questions that might keep the talk going as well as elicit more understanding:

"What do you think made you do that?"
"What was going through your mind at the time?"
"Sounds like something's bothering you today?"
"Why are you worried about this now?"

In print alone, of course, we can't describe the tone of voice that should accompany these questions, but it should be readily apparent that any of the above could be totally ruined by a sarcastic, angry, belittling, condescending, or totally smart alec tone of voice.

Reflecting Feelings

If you are going to tell someone that you think you understand them, it's usually helpful to try to let them know that you can imagine how they must have felt under the circumstances they're describing to you. Sometimes the older kids will tell you that you sound a bit like a shrink. Just say, "Sorry, but I'm just trying to make sure I understand what you're talking about."

In the example above, Mom reflected feelings back at two points:

"That must have been awfully embarrassing."
"Boy, I haven't seen you this mad for a while!"

Other examples of reflecting feelings might include:

"You really sound bummed out about that."
"That must have really been fun!"
"You were pretty upset with me."

Reflecting feelings does a couple of things. It lets the child know that whatever they are feeling is OK (it's what they sometimes do about it that can be wrong). This reinforces self-esteem. It also helps diffuse the feeling so it is not acted out somewhere else. You can bet that if Tom's mother had first said, "That's no way to talk about your teachers!", most of his anger would have been immediately redirected at her.

Perception Checks

The name may sound fancy, but the idea is simple. From time to time during a talk, it is often helpful to check out with the other person whether or not you are "catching their drift," or really getting a good idea of what they're saying. These kinds of comments let you know whether or not you're understanding them correctly, but they also have a second purpose: they tell the child that you're really listening to what they're saying and that you're really trying to see the world for a moment through their eyes.

Examples of checks or summaries might be:

"Sounds like you're saying that our rules for chores favor
  your sister."
"You felt it was your worst day at school this year."
"You're feeling like the new homework arrangement we
  started is working a lot better."
"You wish I weren't gone so much so we could do more
  together?"

Active listening is also an attitude. Your attitude, not your child's. It's the attitude of sincerely trying to figure out what someone else is thinking even if you don't agree or even if it drives you nuts. This, of course, is a different kind of job if you're talking to a two year old or a ten year old, but it's a great self-esteem builder.

And you'll also very often find that, if you listen well, you can learn a lot about what your children think about life.

21

Active Listening
& Counting

I n Chapter 5 of *1-2-3 Magic* we discussed counting and how to use it if the kids are giving you a hard time. Then in Chapter 20 we discussed active listening, and its ability to help diffuse negative emotions. How in the world is a parent supposed to know when to listen and when to count?

If you active listened *all the time*, you wouldn't be any kind of a disciplinarian. Active listening, by itself, has nothing to do with setting limits and enforcing rules. Imagine this scene:

"Mom—you idiot! My best T-shirt's still in the wash!"
"You're feeling pretty frustrated with me."

The parent's response is overly nice and is also inappropriate. The child's disrespect is way out of proportion to the situation and should be confronted.

On the other hand, if you counted *all the time* whenever the kids were upset, you wouldn't be a very understanding parent. Your kids would correctly perceive you as only an instrument of discipline—or worse.

Imagine this common summertime scene:

"I'm bored."
"That's 1."

That's also a pretty insensitive and unnecessary response. Your kids certainly won't want to talk to you very often!

When to count and when to listen? Sometimes it's pretty clear, but often it's not a very easy decision. Here are some guidelines.

If They're Not Upset with *You*

If the child is upset about something that didn't have anything to do with you, it is probably time to active listen. This couldn't be Testing and Manipulation directed at you, because you didn't do anything to frustrate the child.

You're in the family room, for example, and seven year old Jim comes running in from outside yelling:

"THOSE GUYS ARE JERKS!"
"Who's that, Jim?"
"The kids across the street—they won't let me go in their yard."
"Why not?"
"I don't know. They're just morons."
"Boy, you sound really upset!"
"Yeah, I'm not playing with those creeps."
"That sounds like a good idea."

Dad doesn't count the yelling. The problem occurred outside and didn't have anything to do with him, so he figures a little active listening may diffuse the situation.

Or, back to the old summertime refrain (Janie, 10):

"I'm bored."
"You're not having a very good day, huh?"
"No. There's nothing to do."
"You try, but you can't think of anything fun at all?"

"Nope. Can we go get that book I wanted?"

"I've got to go to the mall, anyway. Let's do it."

"All right!"

Mom here doesn't get trapped into making seven suggestions that will be shot down one by one. Her daughter is not feeling too good, but this isn't Badgering or any other type of manipulation. Time for a little sympathy. If they can work out something to do, fine. If not, see the next example.

The Upset Switches *to You*

Sometimes the kids will start out upset by something else, but then their frustration can get switched to the parent. In that case you can still try active listening, but you had better be ready to count.

Janie's situation above is a little tricky. What if Mom doesn't want to do anything or can't go out?

"I'm bored."

"You're not having a very good day, huh?"

"No. There's nothing to do."

"You try, but you can't think of anything fun at all?"

"Nope. Can we go get that new book I wanted?"

"I can't, honey."

"Aw, why not?"

"I've got things to do here."

"What do you have to do?"

"It doesn't make any difference. Plenty. Look, why don't you
    call Megan and see if she wants to do something. I could
    maybe pick her up."

"If you can pick her up, why can't you take me to get my book."

"Better drop it, Janie, or we're going to counting."

"You don't let me do ANYTHING!"

"That's 1."

"THAT'S ONE FOR YOU, TOO!"

"That's 2."

"Oh for pete's sake." (Janie leaves.)

Here Mom tries active listening, but it doesn't diffuse the situation. Janie puts the hit on her to be the local entertainment committee. Mom can't produce the desired services, so Janie gets into Badgering, Martyrdom, and Intimidation. Mom catches herself getting verbally involved in the impossible, and starts counting.

Discuss Problems, Count Attacks

What if the kids are upset with you in the first place? This gets even trickier. It depends some upon how they approach you. In general the rule, "Discuss Problems, Count Attacks," applies.

> "Mom—you idiot—my best T-shirt's still in the wash!"
> "It was filthy dirty, and that's no way to talk to anybody,
>   young man. That's 1."
> "I NEEDED TO WEAR IT THIS AFTERNOON!"
> "That's 2."
> "Jerk!"
> "Take 10, and add 10 more for the mouth."

An attack from the start. Mom did very well. Many parents would give an immediate 3 for the "idiot" remark.

Some things are pretty much attacks, but if a parent uses a little active listening, the emotion may be diffused and things can work out. Mark is ten:

> "Why are you making me do this stupid homework now!?"
> "Homework's a real bummer, isn't it?"
> "Oh, brother." (Mark starts his homework with a sigh.)

Here the active listening helped diffuse the unpleasant emotion so the child didn't act on it. Keep the 1-2-3 ready in your back pocket, though, because you may not always be so lucky:

> "Why are you making me do this stupid homework now!?"
> "Homework's a real bummer, isn't it?"
> "Yeah, I hate it!"

"Boy, you really don't like it, do you?"
"I could be rollerblading with Jason."
"You'd really prefer to be outside playing."
"DON'T JUST SAY BACK EVERYTHING I SAY!"
"That's 1."

Remarkable presence of mind on the part of this parent.

So what's the basic rule? Be ready to discuss problems. But if the child's part of the discussion becomes an attack in the form of Badgering, Threats, Intimidation, whining or some Physical tactic, count.

Part VII:

Over the Years

22

The Family Meeting

When the kids are little, your house should be a dictatorship, and when they are 17 it should be almost, but not quite, a democracy. Obviously, the 1-2-3 is a tactic that doesn't give the kids much say in the discipline. That's the way it should be for the welfare of the children as well as the parents. You decide what is Stop behavior and you punish it with a brief time out, but you do this in a way that is fair, calm, and not emotionally or physically abusive. Charting and other Start behavior tactics are friendlier, but they still are largely designed and applied by you.

Dictatorship to Democracy

Somewhere along the line, however, as the kids get older, you want to begin the evolution toward a more democratic way of conducting business around the house. A good time to start is when the kids are in the primary grades in school. Don't try this when the children are three or four years old, because it will probably just aggravate you and confuse them.

There are several reasons why the Family Meeting is a good idea. As the kids get older—and hopefully more rational—it is more appropriate that they have more say in the things that affect them. Kids also will often cooperate better when they have a say in what's going on. And finally, children need this kind of training for a later time when they have their own families.

The Family Meeting is a good way to start giving the kids more of a voice in household operations. You can use it to discuss not only discipline, but also other issues that come up when people live together, such as laundry, allowances, bedtimes, renting movies, vacations, food, fights, etc. The meetings will be more democratic, but you will still—if necessary—have the final say.

This will mean you'll be doing more talking, but only at the meeting itself. The No-Talking rule will still apply when a rule is being enforced.

The Family Meeting can take place as often as you wish. Once every week or two is ideal, and you can also call special meetings whenever a unique or urgent problem comes up. Kids can request a meeting themselves.

How to Run the Meeting

The format of the meeting is very simple. Mom or Dad (not both at the same time) is the chairperson and has the responsibility for keeping order and staying on task. Older children can take a shot at running the meeting themselves from time to time. The chairperson sees to it that the agenda is followed and that each person gets a chance to speak without being interrupted.

Each person in the family can bring to the meeting a problem that they want resolved. Then the chairperson guides the group through the following steps:

1. One person describes the problem they want resolved.
2. Every other person gives their thoughts and feelings about that problem.
3. Next, the floor is opened for proposals for solutions; anyone can speak, but one at a time.
4. A solution is agreed upon to be tried out. It may combine

different aspects of the suggestions from different people.
If there are disagreements, Mom and Dad have the final say.

5. The agreed upon solution is written down on a piece of paper
   that is posted on the refrigerator, or it can be written in a
   Family Meeting journal or notebook (or computer!).

6. The next person brings up their problem, and steps 2-5 are
   repeated.

All solutions are considered experimental. If they don't work too
well, they can always be reviewed at the next meeting. They should be
concrete, specific, and practical, but sometimes a good deal of creativity
can be exercised in coming up with them.

Sitting through these meetings is not always easy, and it's a good idea
to keep them under an hour so you don't go crazy. Many parents have
agreed that the Family Meeting is one of the *most aggravating and
effective* things you can do with your kids. It sounds contradictory, but if
you can get through the process, people do have a greater tendency to
follow through with the agreed upon solutions. It's also nice that everyone
has a chance to be heard and to learn some negotiation skills—an excellent
preparation for marriage!

Examples

Case 1: Who's been drinking all the pop around here, anyway?

Sandy brings this weighty issue to the Family Meeting. She explains that
Mom usually buys an eight-pack of soda, and there are four people in the
family, but she's not getting her two bottles. There's never any left! The
issue is discussed, with her brother, Mom and Dad throwing in their
opinions. Then a solution is agreed upon.

When an eight-pack enters the house, all bottles will be initialed: two
for Mom, two for Dad, two for Sandy and two for brother. If you drink your
two bottles, you're done. If you want another bottle, you have to check the
eight-pack to see if there's a full bottle and, if so, whose initials are on it.
If there is one, you may purchase it for 50 cents. If the person says no, no

Badgering or Intimidation is allowed. This agreement is then posted on the refrigerator.

Case 2: When is bedtime during the summer?

The kids (ten and twelve) have conspired to bring up at the meeting their opinion that summer bedtime should be different from during the school year. In fact, they don't think they should have a specific bedtime at all during the summer, since they can sleep the next day.

Mom and Dad, incredibly, agree to try it on one condition: if the parents go to bed before kids, the kids have to be amazingly quiet and cannot wake up Mom and Dad at all. Otherwise the deal will be changed.

23

Slipping

Nobody is perfect. Parents and teachers are human beings. They have good days and bad days. Many people have used the 1-2-3 religiously for years and years, but for most of us it is often a struggle to stay consistent and to remember what we're supposed to be doing.

The problem we're talking about here is called "slipping." Some people call it backsliding. It means you start out well, get things shaped up, and then slip back into your previous ways of operating. The 1-2-3 switch sort of goes to the "Off" position. The old status quo has a nasty way of sneaking back up on us. Slipping can occur gradually over a period of months or years, or it can happen more suddenly.

Short Term Slipping

In the course of a day it's easy to get distracted when there's always so much going on. You have to go to work, drive the kids all over the place, cook (or go get fast food), answer junk phone calls, help with homework, call your mother, try to find a little time to read the paper, and so on. When you're trying to do nine things at once, who can remember the No-Talking and No-Emotion rules?

You can! It's not easy, but it beats arguing and screaming, which only add to your troubles, making you feel angry and guilty on top of everything else.

Let's imagine you have just gotten home at 5:30, after having had a hard day at work and picking up one child from soccer and another from piano. Now it's time to make dinner. The kids have been fighting like cats and dogs and you're starting to lose it:

"He's hitting me!"

"I was not! You're a pig!"

"Shut up, you idiot!"

"Knock it off, guys."

"Pig."

"Idiot."

"Now you kids knock it off, YOU HEAR ME! I'm sick and tired of the two of you picking at each other all the time."

"Don't pinch me. DON'T! MOM, he's gonna..."

"DIDN'T YOU GUYS COME WITH EARS?! What did I just say?! That's it, no TV for either one of you tonight."

"That's not fair. I wasn't doing anything." (Cries)

"Ha, ha. You can't watch the moo-vee."

"Neither can you, dummy."

What do you do in this situation? The first thing is to remember that you've forgotten the program. The sooner you catch yourself, obviously, the better. Then do a "mini-Kickoff," telling the kids you're going back to counting. Then shut up and count. In this situation (in the car) a time out can be worth 15 minutes off TV time for the evening.

Let's take it from the top, with Mom or Dad making an effective— though belated—recovery:

"He's hitting me!"

"I was not! You're a pig!"

"Shut up, you idiot!"

"Knock it off, guys."

"Pig."

"Idiot."

"Now you kids knock it off, YOU HEAR ME! I'm sick and
tired of the two of you picking at each other all the time."

"Don't pinch me. DON'T! MOM, he's gonna..."

"OK gang. I'm not doing my job right. We're going back to
counting. As of right now you both are on 1. You guys hit
three, it's 15 minutes off your TV time for tonight. It's up
to you."

"That's not fair. I wasn't doing anything." (Cries)

"Oh, yeah, little Miss Innocent."

"That's 2 for both of you."

(Silence. Both kids pout and stare out car window.)

An NBA referee couldn't have done much better.

Long Term Slipping

You're doing fine with the 1-2-3 and charting, for example, then Mom has
to go into the hospital for a week. Dad stays home and tries to control the
chaos, and when Mom comes home she's still in pain from the surgery.
The kids are nervous and are acting like wild men. You forget the charts
and go back to nagging, arguing, and yelling.

Things get worse and worse. Then about three weeks later, you wake
up in the middle of the night and wonder, "What happened to the 1-2-3?"

Most parents and teachers slip some. There are some who stick to the
straight and narrow forever, but that's not typical. What causes slipping?
The most common causes are:

- Just plain time
- Visitors
- Illness
- Travel
- New babies

For the most part, it seems that any significant disruptions of daily routine
seem to have some potential for causing slipping.

What do you do about slipping? First of all, accept it as normal.
Nobody's perfect, including you, and you shouldn't expect yourself to be.

Life's also a bit more complex than any of us anticipated, especially when it comes to raising children.

Second, it's *back to basics.* Almost invariably, when parents come in and say, "It's not working anymore," what is happening is:

A Violation
of the
No-Talking
and
No-Emotion Rules!

This point cannot be emphasized strongly enough. So we go back and review the theory and the procedures very carefully, and then send Mom and Dad on their way. This usually takes care of the problem.

Fortunately, the Stop and Start behavior training methods described here are simple and can be resurrected and reapplied with little difficulty. The fact that you've used them once and slipped does not hurt their effectiveness the second time around.

Just go back to basics. Turn that 1-2-3 switch to "On."

Over the course of your kids' growing up time with you, you may go through a number of slips and recoveries. Daily, monthly, and annually. That's normal. Each time, catch yourself slipping if you can, pick yourself up, take a deep breath, and go back to what you know works best.

Part VIII:

Counting for Teachers

24

The 1-2-3 in School

Teachers have used the 1-2-3 successfully in the classroom for many years. In fact, in many preschool and grammar schools, the 1-2-3 is the basic discipline system for the entire school. What we have discussed so far is easily adapted to the classroom, and it is done pretty much the same way as parents do it at home.

Some schools use the 1-2-3 in the classroom, and have also trained many of their parents in how to use it at home. This is nice for the children, because they then have the same system in both places, and the consistency makes it easier for them to respond. Like their parents and teachers, the children are happier when there is less hassling about discipline.

This chapter will provide some general information about the application of the 1-2-3 in the school setting. There is room here, however, for a good deal of flexibility and creativity as the 1-2-3 is applied at each different level, so the following chapters will examine how the 1-2-3 can be used in preschool and daycare, in kindergarten through fifth grades, and in a junior high school setting (grades 6 through 8).

Discipline Before Learning

In the classroom some form of order is required if anybody is going to learn anything. Many teachers feel, however, that their training either ignored or only touched on the problem of discipline. Discipline problems are often seen, therefore, as unexpected and unnecessary intrusions into the academic day, rather than as an inevitable—although unpleasant—part of the process of education.

Since there is often little preparation for managing children who have trouble following the rules, a teacher's struggle with the problem may often be a spontaneous reflection of their personality. On the one hand are teachers who have a natural ability to intimidate. Their innate manner communicates clearly that "you don't mess with me." On the other hand are teachers who feel uncomfortable with discipline, and in between are those who have achieved the "happy medium"—those who have the best qualities of each type. Each type has some good and some bad points, and may develop difficulties at different grade levels.

The instructor who is uncomfortable with discipline will have little problem with the children in the early grades, since the children there are usually quite anxious to please the teacher. Problem children—and their parents, however, may be difficult to handle. This teacher may have trouble setting and enforcing limits, especially with older kids, so in junior high or high school they may have an especially difficult time.

The more intimidating sort will also have no problem with the early grades, since the kids wouldn't dream of messing with them. However, this teacher may be tough on the self-esteem of the little ones without knowing it. They will be quite comfortable with setting and enforcing limits, and will often be able to handle junior high and high school kids without suffering too much or hurting anyone else's self-esteem unduly. They may, however, run into battles with problem students and their parents.

Many teachers, of course, develop the happy medium on their own. They have very satisfactory ways of handling discipline without hurting children or being hurt themselves. They can enforce limits effectively, but also can be sensitive and understanding when necessary. However, for those who may be at one extreme or the other, the 1-2-3 can help. For those uncomfortable with discipline, the 1-2-3 gives them a strategy—especially in higher grades. For those who may be too angry or intimidating, the 1-2-3 can help keep them under control, giving them a way of maintaining order without hurting anyone else. And for those who have the happy medium, the 1-2-3 can just make life easier.

The 1-2-3 in the Classroom

Teachers can start using the 1-2-3 anytime, though it is a little easier to get going right from the beginning in September. Usually the teacher will do their version of the Kickoff conversation with the entire class. They then make a list of "countable" offenses, sometimes in a class discussion where the kids help make the list themselves. It is still important to keep in mind the difference between Start and Stop behavior, because the tactics will be different (we'll discuss teachers' Start behavior tactics later).

After the method is discussed, the teacher needs to decide on a consequence for a student receiving a 3. For the preschoolers, kindergartners, and kids through about the third grade, a time out area—usually a chair, table or rug— is chosen. Most teachers like—or are required—to keep the child in the room, rather than out in the hall. For fourth and fifth graders and junior high (6th-8th) students, many—but not all—teachers feel a time out is no longer appropriate, and a consequence such as five or ten minutes subtracted from the student's recess or lunch, or some kind of after school "detention" may be substituted.

For the time out procedure, an area in the back of the room or off to the side is often selected. Some teachers prefer to have the area blocked off visually from the rest of the class by something like a bookcase or file cabinet. A chair or desk can be put in the time out area. If there are two chairs, they shouldn't be too close together and, if possible, should have something between them. There are usually no other materials available, though some teachers will allow children to do schoolwork during the rest period.

When a youngster is acting up, the teacher holds up one finger and says, "John, that's 1." This can be done in front of the class, because if it's done properly the intent is not to embarrass the child. Some embarrassment may be inevitable, but that's not so bad and it goes back to the idea mentioned before: if you don't want to be embarrassed, you can behave. Some teachers get so efficient at counting that they only have to make eye contact with the child and then hold up the appropriate number of fingers. This is often referred to as the "silent finger" approach.

When a child hits 3, they are instructed to go to the time out area. Many teachers simply use a five minute rest period (two or three minutes for the preschoolers), rather than the one minute per year rule. Refusing to go to time out is treated as a major offense, and can be dealt with by a visit to (or from) the principal, a call to the parents, or a restriction of usual school privileges, such as recess or lunch or even the right to go home at 3:15 (detention). Goofing around too much during time out can be handled in a similar fashion. Teachers should tailor the consequences to the child and keep in mind that the more immediate the consequence is, the more effective it usually is.

In some schools, time outs for more serious offenses (or the second or third time out in the same day) are served in the principal's office, but *without* a discussion with the principal. The child simply reports to the office and says they are there for a time out. No one is allowed to talk to them in either a friendly or a reprimanding way. After the required minutes, the student returns to the class.

Like parents, teachers need to keep in mind that kids are not little adults. It is probably true that most adults, when disciplining children, have a tendency to talk and explain things too much. Keep in mind that this is not merely an unfortunate habit. It is very destructive, because it elicits more testing and manipulation, and— even worse—it tends to place the responsibility for the child's good behavior more on the teacher than on the child. Then we have a situation that is more like, "I'll be good if you can talk me into it."

Behavioral Accounting

Teachers have two unique problems that parents don't have, and these make their job somewhat harder. First of all, no parent, as far as we know, has to discipline twenty-five kids at home! The teacher's job, then, becomes keeping track of "who's on first?" What kids are at what counts?

The job is not as daunting as it first appears, however. In a regular classroom on an average day, most children will not be counted at all. In a typical class of twenty-five students, it is unusual if more than three or four kids receive a count of any kind, and on many—or even most—days no one will receive a time out.

Still, some kind of record keeping is necessary and several options are available. Some teachers use the old blackboard routine. With the first count, the child's name goes on the board. The second and third counts result in check marks after the name. If the child goes to 3, the time out is served and the name can be erased. Many teachers feel, however, that the name on the board is too much like "rubbing it in," and at times the names did not get erased when they were supposed to.

Another teacher came up with a more creative idea. She made a big stop light (approximately 24" by 6") out of cardboard, with the usual red light on top, yellow in the middle, and green on the bottom. This was then laminated, and a strip of black vinyl was hung from the bottom. Attached to the vinyl were clothespins, and on each clothespin was the name of a child.

If a child received a count, the child had to get up and move their clothespin from the vinyl to the green light, which stood for a count of 1. The same procedure was followed for a 2 count (clothespin on the yellow light), and finally, if the child hit 3, the clothespin was put on the red light while the time out was served.

Upon leaving the time out area, the kids were then allowed to put their name back on the black vinyl strip.

The nice thing about this setup is that at any one time you can simply glance at the stop light and see where everybody in the class is. On the other hand, the names are not so large and obvious to the whole class as they are when on the board. Other setups using simply big, colored numbers or colored containers (with names on popsicle sticks) can work equally well.

Even with these methods, some teachers feel that less notoriety is better with any behavioral accounting procedure, especially when dealing with the higher grades. One easy method simply involves the teacher writing the student's name on a small note pad when they give the first count or warning. Further counts are then just marked after the name.

Since few kids are usually getting counted in the first place, some teachers just keep the counts in their heads. This shouldn't be done, though, unless it can be done accurately. Keep in mind that many children also keep track—both for themselves as well as classmates—of the counts too, and they may try to correct a teacher who is at the wrong number.

A second issue for teachers is that many rightly feel that the 20 minute rule needs to be modified for the classroom. In other words, they feel that allowing up to three offenses in a twenty minute period, and then going back to a count of zero, makes for too much possible misbehavior in the classroom. What some teachers have done, therefore, is to extend the time during which the counting to 3 continues. Some extend it so it coincides with a usual period (45-50 minutes or so) in the school day. Others have been more strict, and have extended it to the entire morning, with the children then starting again at a count of zero after lunch. In general, most teachers feel that holding the counts over longer periods is more appropriate for older children.

If 1-2-3 Doesn't Solve the Problem

If a child responds to the 1-2-3, but their frequency of problem behaviors stays at an unsatisfactory level, other steps need to be considered. Occasionally, something as simple as moving their seat or some other educational adjustment may help, but often a more extensive look at what is going on becomes necessary.

Some schools use the following sequence:

1. Classroom adjustments (e.g., move seat)
2. Parent conference with teacher (child participates in part of the conference)
3. Parent conference with principal (or assistant principal); restriction of participation in school activities may be considered
4. Social worker or behavioral consultant involved
5. Special services team involved
6. Case study (if not previously done)

These interventions attempt to find out if something else is going on that is causing the child's problem, such as a learning disability, Attention Deficit Disorder, family problems, or other psychological diagnosis (e.g., depression or anxiety).

Classroom Benefits

Over the years teachers have identified a number of important benefits—both for themselves and for their students—that come from using the 1-2-3.

Clear and simple

Teachers feel the 1-2-3 is easy to learn and easy to understand for everyone involved: children, teacher and also parents. Having the rules and disciplinary procedures perfectly clear makes for more order in the classroom. Children respond better when they know exactly what the consequences will be.

Instruction time not wasted

The counting method is crisp and simple enough so that, when done properly, it doesn't waste the valuable and limited amount of time available for learning. Giving a count or warning is done without a lot of chatter, persuasion or arguing. It doesn't have to embarrass or aggravate a youngster, and thus provoke them to counterattack.

Teacher not exhausted by discipline

What about discipline can exhaust a teacher? Two things. One is the useless verbal hassles that you can get caught up with when falling back into the "little adult" assumption. This can lead to nagging and lecturing that tend to produce the "Talk-Persuade-Argue-Yell" (teachers don't usually hit) routine. That's tiring.

The second energy sapping problem is that often when a teacher becomes so involved arguing with one student, the rest of the class goes bananas in a kind of chain reaction. Now the entire class has to be gotten under control.

Discipline with dignity

As one teacher put it, "The 1-2-3 allows us to achieve discipline that maintains the dignity of the students." Misbehavior is handled routinely, and is not treated as if it were the worst thing in the world or some kind of personal insult. The No-Talking and No-Emotion rules see to it that children feel a minimum of "put down" when they are disciplined.

No attention for misbehavior

Some children who have been having problems for a while seem to enjoy causing trouble and being the center of attention. A teacher who talks too much and gets too upset plays right into their hands and actually reinforces the disruptive behavior. The 1-2-3—done properly—does not give undue attention to the wrong things.

Testing & Manipulation identified

We now know the tricks the kids can pull when they are frustrated. The Six Kinds of T&M have been discovered! Life will never be the same for the difficult youngsters who wish to successfully pull off a dose or two of Badgering, Threat or Martyrdom. Teachers find it is very helpful to identify to themselves—right when it is occurring—the kind of testing that is going on. It can then be taken less seriously and also managed effectively.

Do kids test teachers differently than they test their parents? Generally the six types of T&M are the same, but teachers who are also parents of two to twelve year olds often say that in school they get less Intimidation, Threat, and Physical tactics, and more Butter Up. Martyrdom seems to be a favorite in both locations.

On the Playground

Free time and free play outside are times when kids can get into all kinds of hassles. Energy and activity levels are high and there is little structure. Fortunately, children also value their free time a lot, and this makes the 1-2-3 very easy to use for playground supervisors.

If a child is engaging in some kind of Stop behavior, the child is given a 1. It sometimes may have to be shouted a bit, but that's OK as long as the volume is not an expression of anger. If the child hits 3, they must spend five minutes sitting next to the teacher or monitor and just watching the other kids play. Normally they hate that, so they will work hard not to get counted out.

Some teachers like to try something else first when two kids are arguing or fighting. The children are first interrupted. Then they are instructed that they must work out their difference themselves. Often this works. If it doesn't, they are then counted.

Parents and Homework

Teachers are often in the position of having to encourage parents to encourage their children to do their homework. It is a good idea, if you are a teacher, to make it a practice that if you are going to suggest to parents that they "get after" their kids about their homework, that you also suggest some specific ways of doing this. Otherwise, what Mom and Dad may do spontaneously may not be too good, such as nagging, yelling, or interrupting the child in the middle of their favorite TV program.

What are some good methods? Those described in Chapter 15, which include Sloppy PVF, timers and charting, as well as the "Positive-Negative-Positive" method and the "Rough Checkout."

Start Behavior

Start behavior strategies were discussed in Chapter 12. They can all be helpful for teachers, especially Sloppy PVF (positive reinforcement), Kitchen Timers, and Charting. The Docking System can be used sometimes if the class is on a "token economy" type of reward system, but it has more limited application in the classroom, since a teacher is not going to do a child's work for them.

The next chapters will describe how the 1-2-3 has been used in real-life school settings. The descriptions combine some of the best ideas from a number of different educators and from a number of different locations. Two things will become obvious.

First of all, there is not necessarily one right way to apply the 1-2-3.

In some schools, for example, all teachers are required to use it. In other schools some do and others don't. In some preschools and kindergartens, the 1-2-3 is used right off the bat in the beginning of the year, while in others it is used as a "backup" system with extremely difficult classes or difficult students.

Second, the 1-2-3 is only a part of a teacher's behavior management skills. There is much more to running a classroom, and teachers have time and again demonstrated their ingenuity and creativity in coming up with an overall program that includes—but goes beyond—what is covered in this book.

25

Preschool & Daycare

C hildren in preschool and daycare situations—approximately ages two to five—are at the stage where they need to learn basic socialization skills as well as the ability to follow the instructions involved in a daily routine. Parents want their children in these situations to be able to respect the rights of others, to learn to give and take, and to begin to feel good about themselves. They also want their kids to be able to handle a time period of two and one-half or more hours that involves activities such as music, story time, snack time, free play, group sharing time, and arts and crafts.

Good, consistent discipline, obviously, provides a basis for allowing these kinds of learning to occur. If a class of children—no matter how small—is continually out of control and no one gets along, little learning occurs and self-esteem suffers.

Before Using the 1-2-3

Here's one way of handling discipline at this level. Since these children are just learning how to socialize and handle routines, it may not be necessary to start right out with the 1-2-3 (though many schools do). Some preschool or daycare teachers also feel they want to avoid, in the beginning, singling out the child by the counting process. If a child is out of line with their behavior in a group, the first two alternatives can be:

1. Simple distraction: guide or interest the child in another activity
2. Separation from the group for a short time

Little kids are fairly easy to distract, and then the whole problem can be forgotten. If the child needs to be separated from the group, they can sit in a chair or a spot on a rug for a kind of time out period. In one preschool this is done and the child is then allowed to determine when he or she wishes to cooperate and is ready to return to the group. If problems continue, however, for subsequent rest periods the teacher determines when the child will return.

Meeting with Parents

Problems with most children can usually be handled in this way, and the kids eventually learn to follow the rules and the routines. If problems continue beyond this point, then the 1-2-3 will come into play. The teacher and school directors meet with the parents and discuss the child's behavior at school. Teachers also ask, however, about the child's behavior at home, since there are often marked similarities, and they also find out from the parents what kind of discipline they use, who does it, and how the child responds to it.

The idea of this meeting, though, is not to simply identify problems, but also to propose solutions. So after this initial orientation, the *1-2-3 Magic* program is explained to the parents, and the preschool staff emphasize to the parents that the method works especially well if it can be done at both places—home and school. Parents' responses to this are usually fairly positive, since they very likely have also been bewildered by the child's problem behaviors.

Initially in the discussions with parents, emphasis is placed on the No-Talking and No-Emotion rules, on the difference between Start and Stop behaviors, and on being consistent. Parents are required to read the *1-2-3 Magic* book or watch the video, and then they are asked to focus first on Stop behaviors. Teachers explain that Stop behaviors are those that interfere most with the child's ability to socialize, because they cause classmates to shy away from their child. They also explain that—in addition to counting obnoxious behavior—teachers at preschool and the parents at home should also consistently praise any positive behavior the child produces.

Many preschools also tell parents that they will handle the child's behavior during the day, and that the child should not again be held responsible by the parents at home for what happened during the day. In other words, no "double jeopardy." The child would have already received their consequences at school, and the difficult behavior should then be forgotten.

After the parents have read the *1-2-3 Magic* book, a second meeting is held to discuss questions about the program and when it will start. Then the game plan is twofold.

First, parents briefly do the Kickoff conversation (see Chapter 9) at home with the child (or all the children aged 2-12) and then get started— preferably on a weekend.

Second, the preschool teacher talks to the child individually at school and then begins the program at school that same week.

At school the child may be the only one in the class on the 1-2-3 system. When a time out is necessary, a time out chair or rug in the room is used, rather than having the child leave the room. The only time a child will be removed from the room is if they are throwing a temper tantrum that is upsetting the other kids (see explanation below).

After a few weeks, parents (it is important to try to keep Dad involved) and teachers meet again to discuss how the program is going and any bugs in the system. Most schools feel they have great success when the 1-2-3 is implemented properly and consistently both at home and at school.

Other issues discussed in follow up meetings can involve things such as who is responsible for counting (parent or teacher) during the brief period when the child arrives or leaves, or how to train sitters or others who watch the children to use the 1-2-3.

Temper Tantrums

Some kids have a harder time than others at this age in adjusting to new routines, and react with tantrums when frustrated (see testing tactic # 2, Intimidation, in Chapter 10). These can be handled in the following way. First of all, if the tantrum isn't too horrible in the classroom, it can be ignored, and attempts by the child to rejoin the group or activity reinforced.

Second, however, if the tantrum is disturbing other children, the child will have to be removed. They are taken to the rest room (or other unoccupied and confined area with limited distractions), where two teachers or staff stay with the child until the tantrum is over. As the child is yelling or thrashing around on the floor or whatever, one adult periodically tells the child—in a calm and reassuring voice—that they have two choices. They can either continue screaming on the floor and stay in the rest room with the teachers, or they can stop the tantrum and return to the classroom to play with friends. Nothing else is said. Patience is essential!

Preschool teachers have had very good success with *1-2-3 Magic* when it is applied as described here. It helps train—not persuade—the kids, and they can make remarkable gains in maturity over the course of a year. Many preschools and daycare settings prefer to use the 1-2-3 right from the beginning, after only a brief orientation, since the children seem to get the idea at this age more from experiencing the procedure.

Teachers of preschoolers also feel that the 1-2-3 helps reinforce the notion that the behavior is unacceptable, not the child. In addition, the method does not lavish attention on negative behavior. Problem behavior is simply counted in a matter of fact way, which allows the teacher to spend a minimum amount of time on a difficult child. This, in turn, helps the other children to remain positive about that child, rather than starting to avoid them during play.

Elementary Grades (K-5)

N ow we're getting more serious. Not only must children in these years master handling routines, following instructions and getting along with others, but they are also expected to actually learn something. Numbers, letters and other signs of academia start creeping into the day, and the school day is not quite as much fun as it was in preschool. As the years progress, the daily demands to sit still and pay attention to more and more difficult tasks increase dramatically. None of this can develop as it is supposed to if class discipline is weak and behavior is out of line.

Kindergarten

Kindergarten is kind of an "in between" year. The day is still short and the children are still allowed to move around a lot. On the other hand, it is common that kindergartners will be expected, by year end, to recognize and to write their ABCs, to be able to count to one hundred, to recognize and write the numbers up to about twenty or so, and to be able to recognize a few short words.

Kindergartners are also very sensitive at this age, their feelings can be easily hurt, and they see the teacher as a kind of god. Many have learned a lot about handling the demands of a daily routine in preschool. This often makes the discipline task easier in general for many teachers.

Teachers' personalities and skills vary considerably, however. Some have a quality about them that automatically communicates "you don't fool around in here," while others appear more anxious and less intimidating. Classes also vary more than the law of averages would seem to dictate. Some years the kids are a breeze to teach, and then there are the "classes from hell" that everyone dreads getting.

What this boils down to is this: for kindergarten some teachers will lean more toward the preschool methods described in the last chapter, where the 1-2-3 is used more as a backup method that kicks in only with more difficult children. Other kindergarten teachers, however, who may not be naturally intimidating or who may be dealing with a very difficult class, may prefer the 1-2-3 method described below for the primary grades.

Getting the Year Started

It will usually take two weeks or less to get the kids oriented to the 1-2-3 discipline system. If children are third graders, of course, and they've been doing the 1-2-3 for the last two years, it will be easier for them. But for new kids in any grade, kindergartners and first graders it is important to go over the procedures daily for the first two weeks.

During the first week the teacher does this in detail each day (what is explained will be covered in the next section). During the second week, class discussions are geared toward the children telling the teacher how the system works. This helps the teacher know how well the class understands the 1-2-3 and what kids may be having trouble grasping it.

Other methods that have been used to orient children to the 1-2-3 include actually showing part of the *1-2-3 Magic* video. One of the best parts is the "twinkie example" showing the little girl testing her mother in the kitchen. Some teachers have also used role playing. After explaining the 1-2-3 and also describing the different kinds of Testing and Manipulation, the teacher has selected students demonstrate the different testing tactics. The teacher—or a student playing the teacher—then counts them.

Parents are oriented primarily in two ways. On the first day of school a note is sent home describing the discipline program and the classroom rules. This note is to be signed (preferably by both parents) and returned. This helps to make sure that the parents understand the system and that they have agreed to it. This is also very helpful if a later parent conference is required about behavioral problems.

The second part of parent orientation is a parent night, which should be held not later than the second week of school. As part of this program, the discipline procedures are again explained to the parents, and comments and questions are encouraged. Usually the *1-2-3 Magic* book and video are shown as references at the parent night, and parents are encouraged to borrow them to familiarize themselves with the program. Parents are told very clearly that it is in the children's best interests that the 1-2-3 be used both at school and at home.

Using the 1-2-3

Four or five important classroom rules, such as "Follow Directions," "Be a Friend," and "Listen Carefully," can be posted on the wall in the classroom. During the first two weeks the teacher will have explained what these rules mean and what will be counted. Common behaviors counted at this age include getting out of your seat, forgetting to raise your hand, arguing or fighting with someone, pushing in line, talking at the wrong time, and tattling.

Many teachers will also count "attitude." This can include excessive expressions (verbal or nonverbal) of disrespect or excessive pouting (see Chapter 8, Variations).

The teacher has explained that if a rule is broken, the child will be given the first warning, "That's 1." If the class is using the stoplight, the student must move their clothespin from below the stoplight and put it on green, or 1 (see description of stoplight in Chapter 24). A second incident will bring a 2 and the child moves the clothespin again (to yellow). Kids are usually embarrassed having to get up to move the clothespin, so this in itself acts as a deterrent to further misbehavior.

The third occurrence of a problem receives a "That's 3, take 5" from the teacher. Nothing else is said. The child moves their marker to 3 (red). They then serve a five minute time out on a "time out rug" which is located off to one side of the classroom. Five minutes is a good length of time for kids this age, rather than exactly one minute per year of their age. For the little ones who do not tell time yet, they are instructed to just pay attention to the movement of the big hand on the clock. They are responsible for telling when the time out is up, moving their marker back down, and returning to their seat.

For children this age, getting a time out is a big deal. Many of the little ones will become teary if they are counted at all, but especially if they are counted to 3. Part of this is simply due to embarrassment, and this is not bad or harmful. It is part of how kids learn and is par for the course. The teacher should ignore the tears. The stoplight on the wall also gives a constant reminder of where everybody stands with regard to counting.

For the purposes of the 1-2-3, the school day is divided into two parts, morning and afternoon. For the kindergartners, of course, there is just one part, morning or afternoon. Warnings can add up to three during the entire morning (or afternoon), but at lunchtime everyone returns to zero and starts fresh. A child, for example, might get a 1 at 9:30 AM, a 2 at 11 AM, and a 3 at 11:40.

Kids like the idea of starting fresh in the morning each day, and starting over each afternoon. Keep in mind, however, that in a typical class most kids will probably not be counted at all on an average day. On a typical day fewer than 20% of the children will receive a count at all, and fewer than that, of course, will receive a time out.

Counting can also be done in special classes, such as music, art, gym, and computers. Those counts are usually kept separately from the regular classroom discipline program, due to the difficulty involved in communicating them back to the main classroom teacher.

For Bigger Trouble

For children who do have more trouble keeping themselves in line, the following procedures can be used:

1st time out: lose sticker
2nd time out: note or phone call to parents
3rd time out: meeting with parents, principal, and teacher

Stickers can be used as part of a charting system. Each child can earn a sticker, for example, by going the whole day without getting a time out. At the end of the day, the kids put their stickers on the chart. The chart is placed on a wall, bulletin board, fire escape door or whatever. On the chart each child has a spot where they place their own creation for the month. This might be a brightly colored picture of a leaf, a pumpkin, a bucket, or whatever, and the sticker goes there.

As it is at home, kids up to the ages of eight or nine like the daily stickers, and this helps reinforce good behavior at the end of each day. The stickers can also tie into a class reward. In the beginning of each calendar month, the class decides what reward or treat it would like to work for. It might be something like twenty minutes free time, a video, a pizza party at lunch, making ice cream sundaes, and so on. The reward takes place on the first day of the next month—if it is earned.

The teacher explains that to earn the reward, every child in the class must get at least fifteen stickers for the month. The average month may have slightly more than twenty school days in it, so this system does not require perfection. This is important because of the children who do have more difficulty controlling themselves.

This does mean, though, that the children who do have more behavioral difficulties will get some heat from other class members to stay in line or shape up. Reprimands from classmates, such as "Joey, you're gonna lose our treat," may be heard from time to time, and they may be met with defiance or pouting, but they usually do help their receiver to self-control. Occasionally, the classroom teacher may need to count the reprimanders, though, if they are becoming too self-righteous and nagging.

Counting the Whole Class

There are those days in a teacher's life when everybody seems to be going nuts at the same time. Everyone—kids and staff— seems to be more flaky during the days right before a vacation or near the end of the school year. And then there are some classes that are just more difficult in the first place.

At times, therefore, it may be helpful to count the entire class. The teacher says, "Class, that's 1 for everyone," or "If this doesn't stop, I'm going to have to count the whole class." After giving a count, of course, the teacher says nothing and stands quietly watching the class. What if the class hits 3? There's not enough room on the rug for twenty-five bodies, so one alternative is to simply have the children put their heads down on their desks for five minutes. This helps calm them down anyway. Then the teacher states when the time out is up, and the class continues with it's discussion or next activity.

Counting the entire class can be tied into the class reward if necessary. For example, the third time in any one month that the whole class is timed out cancels the treat. Watch out if this occurs early in the month!

The procedure for counting the class, of course, should be explained to the children and the parents at the beginning of the school year. Two problems with counting the whole class should be kept in mind. First of all, many teachers use this only as a last resort, since it sometimes makes everyone feel bad. Second, there are almost inevitably children who are not really misbehaving who will get counted along with the class, and they will feel this procedure is unfair, but class time outs are not usually counted on an individual student's record.

Start Behavior Tactics

The main Start behavior strategies used in the classroom include Sloppy PVF, timers, and charting.

Sloppy PVF (positive verbal feedback) is very important to little children and can have a big impact on their behavior. Teachers are often both very aware of this fact and also very good at praising their young charges on a regular basis, so we don't need to elaborate here a lot. A few points might be helpful.

In Chapter 12, we explained that praise should be tailored to the child. Some kids like it "syrupy" and some kids go more for the business-like kind. The rule here is: tailoring is more and more of a consideration the older the kids get. The little ones in kindergarten and first grade usually do fine with the more effusive reinforcement.

Praise can be directed not only toward individual kids, but also at the whole class or at separate work groups or teams. The praise should be very specific. "The red table is really working hard today. Everyone has their pencil in their hand, their eyes on their papers, and they're working quietly."

With the younger children "next door" or "across the room" praise can often be used to help a child who is off task or misbehaving. Imagine Jimmy is staring out the window when he's supposed to be writing his numbers to ten. Right next to him, Sarah is working diligently. Out loud in front of the class teacher says, "I'm really impressed with how hard Sarah is working. Her pencil is in her hand and she's writing very neatly." Jimmy is reminded of the task without being embarrassed.

A teacher should always have a supply of a few kitchen timers. For people who don't like the ticking, hourglasses can be found in sand, liquid, or LCD versions. Timers can be used from time to time for students who tend to daydream instead of work. They can be used to help along clean up times or other occasions where the whole class must get ready for something. They can also be used to time time outs.

Charting is always a friendly way of motivating the children to do what they're supposed to, and classrooms often have a number of charts on the wall. The little children like stickers that are colorful and interesting, and older kids are also interested in something that keeps a detailed record of their performance (like a gradebook!).

The only problem with charting in the classroom is that it takes time. If at the end of the day, for example, all children who had no time outs get to put their sticker on their chart, class time is used up, so the teacher must feel that this is a useful activity and set aside the time. One group or row of children can go up at one time. Just as it is with parents, it is important to keep up with the charting (the kids usually help with frequent reminders). Even then, the charts may need to be varied every few months or so so the children stay interested in them.

Benefits and Problems

Teachers have found that having an orderly, kind and fairly aggressive system of discipline such as *1-2-3 Magic* helps a tremendous amount in maintaining an orderly class. Most children also seem to like it. Children encountering special difficulties such as Attention Deficit Disorder, learning disabilities or even temporary family crises, also find it gives them something concrete and consistent to relate to.

Teachers have also commented that they like the idea of the two warning counts, rather than an immediate punishment. This gives the children a chance to shape up—and to be rewarded for that. Many teachers also feel the 1-2-3 is a control on them—giving them something concrete to do and preventing them from getting unnecessarily angry or upset.

As parents have found at home, though, the 1-2-3 only works well in the classroom if it is done consistently. Being human, many people find themselves reminding the kids about a rule rather than first counting. "Julie, the rule is you must raise your hand first." This is not a big problem. What is a big problem, however, is giving the same child a second reminder instead of counting. This will encourage misbehavior and talking, and it will waste class time.

Some teachers have also found that parent pressure affects their use of the 1-2-3. Some parents can be aggressive and seem to feel that their child can do no wrong. The child pouts and gets teary when counted out, tells the parents, and they then question the teacher about their methods. The teacher feels a little intimidated and starts reminding the child more, instead of counting, and also lets the child hold at 2 when a count of 3 has really been earned. Over a period of time—and not too long at that—this child's behavior will almost certainly deteriorate.

Junior High (6-8)

In grades six through eight—often called junior high—the going gets tougher for the teacher. The kids have long since ceased to see the teacher as some kind of god who can do no wrong. They are also feeling the first stirrings of you know what—adolescence! And in our society today, it certainly seems that adolescence comes earlier and earlier.

Welcome to Adolescence!

Adolescence means the kids want to be—or at least look like they are—more independent from their teachers and parents. They are also starting to identify more with their peer group than with adults or family, and in grades six through eight they are more and more experiencing the great teenage need to be different. That means different from you the adult, not necessarily from each other (adults don't often wear baseball caps backwards).

Adolescence is probably the time in your life when your social sensitivity is at is highest. Adolescents, therefore, do not take well to being humiliated in public. For this reason, many will not act up in a classroom

169

in the first place. Others, however, may be willing to take on a teacher in front of the class if they feel they are being embarrassed. Their feeling is "I will not lose to you" or "I will not let you make me look like an idiot with all these people watching." This attitude gets even stronger if the student feels—rightly or wrongly—that a teacher's discipline is unfair or that it represents their simply grinding their own axe at the student's expense.

Compounding the problem is the fact that in many junior highs each student may have six or seven different teachers during the day, each for a period of about fifty minutes. Many teachers feel that the combination of more teachers per day and incipient adolescence can make for more acting out in class. Team teaching may help, but it is still harder for any one teacher to keep track of the behavior and academic skills of so many students.

Whatever a teacher does with regard to discipline, it is likely that many students at this level will feel it is stupid. A natural part of adolescent psychology is the automatic tendency to question the actions of adults. And after all, what can you reasonably expect adolescents to say about a discipline system of any kind?

Classroom order must still be maintained, however, and some way of keeping track of misbehavior is necessary. Teachers have some difference of opinion about using the basic 1-2-3 procedure in grades six through eight. Some teachers have done it pretty much the same way as it is done in the primary grades. They hold up one finger and say "That's 1" for a warning, and at 3 the student takes a time out in a time out area. One teacher had the youngster actually sit on the floor in the doorway to the room.

Other teachers, however, feel that holding up one finger and saying "That's 1" is too "juvenile" or too much of a "put down" for kids this age. As a matter of fact, in some ways we agree—that's part of the reason why the 1-2-3 system is recommended for use with kids up to around age twelve (approximately sixth grade age), and the *Surviving Your Adolescents* program is used after that.

On the other hand, home and school are not the same, and children are usually likely to test and push their parents more than their teachers. It may also be true that—even with junior high kids—the perception of a "put down" in any discipline may have more to do with the way something is said, rather than the actual words. When the 1-2-3 is done properly, with no extra verbiage and no unnecessary emotion, it is not in any way an attempt to humiliate. That does not always mean, of course, that it will be perceived that way.

What to Do

What it boils down to, then, is this. Some junior high teachers will be able to do the 1-2-3 just as it is done in the earlier grades. These will probably be the teachers who are very comfortable setting and enforcing limits, who do a minimum of talking about discipline, and who do not upset easily or act as though discipline were a form of revenge.

Other teachers may do best to modify several things: the "silent finger" routine, the language and the consequence. Instead of holding up one finger or two fingers when giving a warning, the warnings are simply given verbally. This must be done efficiently, however, because it temporarily breaks the flow of whatever else the teacher is saying.

Second, the language of the warning can be changed, though it should still include the 1-2-3 concept, i.e., the third time you do something disruptive or out of line, there will be a consequence. Possible warnings might include:

"John, I'm going to have to give you your first warning."
"This is the first time I'm going to ask you to stop."
"This is your second reminder."
"We're on the second time now, Sue."
"That's the third one, Matt."
"I'm afraid that's strike three, Julie."

Third, the consequence that occurs with the third incident can be modified. Possibilities at the equivalent of 3 include a visit to the assistant principal, a reduction of free time (e.g., lunch) or other daily enjoyable activity (a kind of time out served in the office), or a detention (time served at the end of the school day).

Some of these consequences are delayed, of course, but they may not lose their impact because the kids are older and more able to associate the offense with the consequence. It cannot be emphasized enough, however, that the power of any deterrent will be minimized if it is presented with excessive anger or an attitude of vengefulness. Adolescents will quickly sense that a "game" is in the air, and many will then play it with gusto. This is not only very disruptive for the entire class, but it is also very discouraging and exhausting for the instructor.

Keeping Track

When a student has five to seven different teachers and the consequences involve something that takes place at a different time and outside the classroom, record keeping becomes a necessary evil. Teachers must also coordinate with the main office regarding exactly what a student has done and what consequence they are subject to. Any record keeping must be as simple and clear as possible, because it will be time consuming. The computers and data base software programs available today can help greatly with this process, but it does require considerable staff time.

Two things can be helpful here: a "Behavioral Accounting Form" (or discipline slip) and a "Behavioral Accounting (or "Step") System." The same Behavioral Accounting Form can be used by the classroom teacher for two purposes: to keep track of what student is at what point and to inform the office of what happened. It needs to be brief, so that filling it out does not disrupt class time unnecessarily.

Here's one possibility. The teacher fills in what the student did that generated each warning, such as talking, being out of one's seat, bothering someone else, etc. This is done right in class and right after the action occurred, but it is done in a calm, unobtrusive, and unchallenging manner. The "3rd Occurrence" is no longer a warning since it nets the consequence. If the student is to report to the office, they take the slip with them to give to the assistant principal.

The form might look something like this:

Behavioral Accounting Form

Date:.............................

Student's Name:...

1st Warning: _____

2nd Warning: _____

3rd Occurrence: _____

Teacher Signature:...

The Behavioral Accounting System is kept by the main office and provides an orderly way for keeping track of the disciplinary history of each student. Incidents that occur represent "steps" on a progressive discipline and intervention program. It is important to keep in mind here that the purpose of such a system is evaluative and corrective, not primarily punitive. Any student who is continually running into trouble needs to be disciplined, but their life may also need to be examined more closely to try to determine what is going wrong.

The Behavioral Accounting or Step System provides for both discipline and evaluation. Each time an incident occurs, the student "progresses" to another defined point on the system, which serves the purpose of being a consequence (inevitably unpleasant). Each point, however, also defines an evaluation and planning function. Information is gathered about what might be happening to cause the trouble and an attempt is made to make plans to alleviate the problems. A student can progress slowly (one step at a time) by accumulating "minor" infractions (e.g., tardies, referrals from class), or quickly (to the next "major" step) by engaging in more serious activities (e.g., fighting, smoking in school, etc.). A student can also receive an automatic 3 in class (skipping 1 and 2) and a "major" referral by doing something that the teacher considers to be very serious in the first place.

Here's what the Behavioral Accounting System might look like:

Step System

Minor Steps
    1 (Minor consequence)
    2   "
    3   "
    4   "

Major Step: 5
    • Meeting with student, parents and Assistant Principal
    • Plan for addressing problem

Minor Steps
    6 (Minor consequence)
    7   "

Major Step: 8
    • Meeting with student, parents and Assistant Principal
      or Principal
    • Meeting of teacher team
    • Involvement of Special Services Team
    • Plan for addressing problem

Minor Steps
    9 (Minor consequence)
    10   "

Major Step: 11
    • Case Study or other thorough evaluation

The above system is a general plan for discipline, and it can be modified by each school as it sees fit. It is also a good idea for the plan to be explained in the beginning of the school year and published in some kind of student handbook. The idea of "progressing" on the step system is itself something of a deterrent to students.

Students can go back "down" on the Step System by going ten school days without any incident occurring. A student at Step 9, for example, can go back to Step 8. The interventions listed above, of course, do not kick in as the student goes back down. Most kids like the idea of this kind of positive reinforcement, and it also reduces their vulnerability to more "intrusive" interventions. Although it is beyond the scope of this book, a step system like this has been also used successfully at the high school level.

Part IX:

Final Thoughts

28

The Payoff

N ow that you know what the 1-2-3 is all about, it's time to get started. You have lots of company. To date the 1-2-3 has been used by hundreds of thousands of parents in all fifty states—not to mention a number of foreign countries. It has also been used successfully in schools, preschools, and daycare centers. Community mental health centers also integrate the 1-2-3 with their evaluation and treatment of children's problems. In one mental health center, for example, parents of young children who call for an appointment attend a two-part 1-2-3 workshop before they ever see a therapist. After completing this brief training program, approximately 80% of the parents do not feel they need further services.

1-2-3 Magic is known for producing results. It works—and it often works in a very short period of time. No magic. Just the logical, consistent application of certain basic principles to the Nth degree.

What can you expect if you decide to use the 1-2-3 at home? You can expect a more peaceful household, with a lot less arguing and fewer angry moments. There will be more time for fun, and affection will come more easily. The self-esteem of your children will improve, and so will your self-esteem as a parent, because you will be more effective, more in control, and you will know you are handling things correctly. If you are a teacher, you will feel more confident, more in control of your class, and your will have more time for instruction.

Parents have often said the 1-2-3 works "like magic." That's where we got the title. What do the kids say about it? Many children say they don't like it, and the reason, of course, is that they are not getting their way as much as they did before.

But—more importantly—many more children have said they like the 1-2-3. When asked why, they say, "Because Mom and Dad don't yell so much." That's a very meaningful statement. It's essential for parents to be in charge of their homes, but it's also crucial that they do this in a way that is not emotionally or physically harmful to their children.

So, it's time to get going with the Kickoff Conversation. Begin by using the 1-2-3 on Stop behavior: do the counting for a week or two to get things under control, and then add the Start behavior techniques. Don't be naive. Get yourself ready for some good, old fashioned Testing and Manipulation.

The 1-2-3 works—if you do it. Things could be quite different at your house—or in your classroom—in a very short period of time. Good luck in your efforts!